Transforming America

A Voter's Bill of Rights

WILLIAM JOHN COX

USVRA.US
A California Nonprofit Corporation
http://www.usvra.us

ISBN 13: 9781519757920
ISBN 10: 1519757921

ALSO BY WILLIAM JOHN COX

Hello: We Speak the Truth
You're Not Stupid! Get the Truth: A Brief on the Bush Presidency
Mitt Romney and the Mormon Church: Questions
Target Iran: Drawing Red Lines in the Sand
The Holocaust Case: Defeat of Denial
The Book of Mindkind: A Philosophy for the New Millennium
Sam: A Political Philosophy
An Essential History of China: Why it Matters to Americans
Millennial Math & Physics

TABLE OF CONTENTS

Dedication

To the People of the United States of America,
Whose consent to be governed,
Cannot be taken for granted.

"As it is my design to make those that can scarcely read understand,
I shall therefore avoid every literary ornament and put it in language as plain as the alphabet."
Thomas Paine, *Common Sense*, (1776)

THE UNITED STATES VOTERS' RIGHTS AMENDMENT

Section 1.

The right of all citizens of the United States, who are eighteen years of age or older, to cast effective votes in political elections is inherent under this Constitution and shall not be denied or abridged by the United States or by any State.

Section 2.

Equality of rights under the law shall not be denied or abridged by the United States or by any State on account of sex.

Section 3.

The States shall ensure that all citizens who are eligible to vote are registered to vote.

In balancing the public benefit of maximum voter participation with the prevention of voting fraud, Congress and the States shall not impose any unjustifiable restriction on registration or voting by citizens.

The intentional suppression of voting is hereby prohibited and, in addition to any other penalty imposed by law, any person convicted of the intentional suppression of voting shall be ineligible for public office for a period of five years following such conviction.

Section 4.

The rights protected by the Constitution of the United States are the rights of natural persons only.

Artificial entities established by the laws of any State, the United States, or any foreign state shall have no rights under this Constitution and are subject to regulation by the People, through Federal, State, or local law.

The privileges of artificial entities shall be determined by the People, through Federal, State, or local law, and shall not be construed to be inherent or inalienable.

Section 5.

Federal, State and local government shall regulate, limit, or prohibit contributions and expenditures, to ensure that all citizens, regardless of their economic status, have access to the political process, and that no person gains, as a result of their money, substantially more access or ability to influence in any way the election of any candidate for public office or any ballot measure.

Federal, State and local government shall require that any permissible contributions and expenditures be publicly disclosed.

The judiciary shall not construe the spending of money to influence elections to be speech under the First Amendment.

Section 6.

Nothing contained in this article shall be construed to abridge the freedom of the press, which includes electronic and digital publication.

Section 7.

In balancing the public benefits of corruption-free elections with allowing candidates to accept private campaign contributions, Congress and the States shall favor public financing over private contributions.

Broadcasters using the public airwaves shall provide free airtime for political campaign programming; ensure controversial issues of public importance are presented in an honest, equitable and balanced manner; and provide equal time to opposing candidates and political points of view.

No campaign for elective public office, including receipt of campaign contributions, shall commence prior to six months before such election.

Section 8.

Election districts represented by members of Congress, or by members of any State legislative body, shall be compact and composed of contiguous territory. The State shall have the burden of justifying any departures from this requirement by reference to neutral criteria such as natural, political, or historical boundaries or demographic changes. Enhancing or preserving the power of any political party or individual shall not be such a neutral criterion.

Congress shall apportion the number of representatives according to the decennial census to ensure the representation of a maximum of 250,000 Persons in each district.

Section 9.

It shall be a primary function of the government to ensure that the People are supplied with truthful, unbiased, objective, and timely information regarding the political, economic, environmental, financial, and social issues that affect them, and that all students are educated in the nature and responsibilities of representative democracy.

The University of the United States shall be established to incorporate all federal service academies and to provide education on the nature and responsibilities of representative democracy, the meaning of freedom, and the appropriate limitations on the use of coercion and force.

Section 10.

During the calendar year preceding a presidential election, Congress shall solicit public comment regarding the political issues that most concern the People.

Prior to the end of the calendar year preceding a presidential election, Congress shall adopt a joint resolution articulating questions regarding the twelve most critical policy issues to be addressed by the next president and Congress.

Failure of Congress to adopt such a joint resolution prior to the end of such calendar year shall result in the disqualification of all sitting members of Congress to be eligible for reelection.

Section 11.

Federal elections conducted every second year shall be held on a national voters' holiday, with full pay for all citizens who cast ballots.

Federal elections shall be conducted on uniform, hand-countable paper ballots and, for the presidential election, ballots shall include the twelve most critical policy questions articulated by Congress, each to be answered yes or no by the voters.

Paper ballots shall provide space allowing voters to hand-write in their choice for all elective federal offices, if they choose, and all such votes shall be counted.

Section 12.

Clauses Two and Three of Article Two, Section One and the Twelfth and Twenty-third articles of amendment to the Constitution of the United States are hereby repealed.

Clause Four of Article Two, Section One of the Constitution of the United States is amended to read as follows: "The Congress shall determine the dates of the primary and general elections of the president and vice president, which dates shall be the same throughout the United States. The presidential and vice presidential candidates receiving the most popular votes by all citizens of the United States shall be elected."

Section 13.

No person, having previously served as an official of the federal government, whether elected, appointed, employed, or serving in the military shall engage in any employment to advocate an interest or position to any Government official for a period of time following such service equal to the period of such service.

No person advocating an interest or position to any government official, whether or not for pay, shall offer or provide any campaign contribution, gifts, or things of value, including favors, services, travel, meals, entertainment, honoraria, and promises of future employment to such government official, nor shall such official accept any such proffering.

Restrictions imposed on such persons by this section shall not be deemed to violate the rights of free speech or petition for redress.

Section 14.

No member of Congress, federal judge, or federal official shall vote, or rule on any matter in which such person or their spouse, domestic partner, child, or contributor of more than minor amounts of campaign funds has a financial, legal, or beneficial interest.

Section 15.

This article shall be inoperative unless it shall have been ratified as an amendment to the Constitution by conventions in the several States, as provided in the Constitution.

Delegates to State conventions to ratify this amendment shall be selected by special elections held within three months of its being proposed by Congress to the States. The voters in each congressional district in the several States shall elect one delegate. All delegate candidates shall affirm under oath when filing as a candidate whether they will vote yes or not for ratification of the proposed amendment, and their position shall be printed with their names on the special election ballot. Delegates shall not have the power to vote differently than their stated intention.

Conventions shall be held in the capitals of each State within three months of the election of delegates, with the chief justice of the highest court in the State chairing the convention. Tie votes by delegates shall be considered a vote for ratification.

The power of delegates convened pursuant to this section shall be restricted to voting yes or no for ratification of the proposed amendment. Such conventions shall not have the power to make changes to the proposed amendment or to consider other constitutional amendments.

The costs of ratification pursuant to this section shall be an expense of the federal government.

PREFACE

Americans are facing a crisis! A review of the mass media produces an abundance of critical commentary telling us why it has happened and who is to blame, yet it reveals a dearth of new ideas and solutions. There is no shortage of pundits of every political stripe, who are quite clever at tearing down their opposition. Few, however, speak with the insight of those who founded the United States of America, the first republic in history created with the consent of the People and based upon a written constitution, which defined and limited its government.

Riding the intellectual wave of the Enlightenment, a small group of gifted thinkers came together in the English colonies of America to organize a government for the benefit of those whom it governed. Working together and often in competition, the founders wove the fabric of freedom which has clothed and protected the American People from abusive government for more than two centuries. That system of consensual representative democracy has endured and has been a model for others around the world to define their own form of self-government.

Although it has evolved to allow the votes of most citizens, the government of the United States no longer provides for the "general welfare" of those who elect it, nor does it protect their interests. Indeed, it has come to pose a danger to its own people and to those of other nations. Continuation of the People's consent to that government depends on whether it can peacefully evolve to meet the needs of the People and to present less of a threat to our society.

What follows is based on two realities. The first is that We, the People of the United States of America do not presently have a constitutional right to vote. The other is that we should withdraw our consent to be governed, until such time as our right to cast effective votes is clearly established in our Constitution.

Each of you who reads or listens to these words was born with the innate capacity to learn and to think for yourself. Some of you received more education, while others have had greater opportunities in life to consider the social, political, economic, and environmental threats of our time. Most of you have formed opinions about some or all of these matters, resulting in a natural resistance to contrary ideas. Many of you rely on religious principles to guide your choices, while others reject such beliefs. Each of you, however, has the present ability to reflect upon these words, and to make up your own mind regarding their value in helping you make beneficial decisions about your life and the society you live in.

The time has come for the People of the United States of America to peacefully transform our government to finally achieve an effective democratic republic, to fairly represent all of the People and to restrain its dangerous and destructive power. It is easy to identify what is wrong—the crucial and more difficult question is how to make it right.

Short of a violent revolution, there is only one power left to the People, which can make a difference. We the People literally hold the power in our own hands: it is our individual vote, and the manner in which we choose to exercise it.

Our vote can be withheld, which simply abdicates our power, or our vote can be expressed in a nonviolent rebellious spirit—as a physical demonstration of our intelligence, literacy, creativity, and responsibility.

Voters have the ability and the power to thoughtfully answer vital political questions on paper ballots and to establish the policies of our nation, and we can carefully write in the names of those we choose to represent us in carrying out our policies. Our vote must be relevant to the real problems that confront us, and it must be effective in leading to solutions of those problems.

A representative democracy requires responsible voting. If the American people continue to cast ill-conceived computerized votes on unreliable machines in response to the latest 30-second political attack ad on television or shock jock diatribe on talk radio, we are being played as pawns in a game we cannot win. If we do not take personal responsibility for our individual vote, we are failing ourselves and our posterity.

The reality of our circumstance leaves us with no choice but to take action. In doing so, we must respect the efforts of those who laid the intellectual foundation of our republic, and we have to avoid the errors of the past. Not only must we honor those who fought for our freedoms, but we also have to accept the duty of the suffrage earned by their sacrifice, and to cast informed votes of wisdom and conscience.

Voting must become the political religion of the nation, celebrated on a paid holy day of reflection and consecrated through the sacrament of voting at the altar of freedom.

We must open our minds to new ideas and different ways to govern ourselves. Americans have to rationally examine the political and social crisis of our time and once again arrive at an enlightened solution. Rather than restoring something lost, we must transform our government in order to finally achieve its promise.

The lamp of liberty must be refueled to continue lighting the way for all of humanity in our universal quest for peace. We must create a better and happier life for our children, who will remain, along with the problems we fail to solve, once we depart our earthly existence.

The Illumination of Rights

A very long time ago, before there were kings and before there was organized religion, people were basically equal. Then something happened, and for thousands and thousands of years, the combination of royalty and religion controlled and manipulated the lives of everyone they conquered and converted.

There were periods in ancient Greece and Rome when certain classes of people had a vote in their government, but most of the time throughout the Dark and Middle Ages, monarchs ruled, religions enabled, the aristocracy supported, and everyone else existed for the benefit of king and church. Ordinary people—commoners—had no role in government, such as it was. They were little more than a part of the property they inhabited. They were without rights.

The West was plunged into a dark abyss of ignorance, and were it not for the flourishing of Chinese and Islamic cultures, the intellectual progress of humanity would have been reset to zero.

Beginning with the Italian Renaissance in the Fourteenth Century, continuing through the Religious Reformations of the Sixteenth, and the Enlightenment of the Seventeenth and Eighteenth Centuries, advances in art, literature, science, religion, economics, and education compelled a substantial change in Western society. Primary among the inventions of the period was the printing press, the progenitor of information technology.

Astronomers perfected telescopes to rediscover the place of the earth in the solar system; mathematicians created new tools to reveal the laws of the universe; doctors and scientists studied human anatomy and physiology and discovered medicinal and surgical cures for diseases; explorers ventured across surrounding oceans; and capitalism and banking took root in the economy.

Sovereignty and Political Power

Monarchies were united, countries were formed, and wars were fought. States, defined by geographic boundaries, were created to concentrate administrative and military power in the sovereign. The measure of a king became his ability to raise money and armies to fight wars. The definition of a state became its capacity to outlast its rulers.

The nobility contributed to the armies of Western monarchs and collected the taxes. In time, the aristocrats gained the power to impose some limitations on their sovereigns and to have a say in how they were ruled.

Once William of Normandy conquered England, he established a council of land owners and church leaders to advise him on making laws. Two hundred years later, the landed aristocracy forced King John to sign the Magna Carta, which restricted his ability to impose taxes without the council's consent. England's parliamentary system and unwritten constitution evolved from this beginning.

Following the English Civil War and the return of Charles II to the throne in 1660, Parliament seized the power to regulate the economy. This included supervision of corporations, such as the East India Company, and trade with the American colonies. The accumulation of wealth provided political and social power and paved the way for bankers, insurers, industrialists, and businessmen to enter government and the nobility.

Economic competition inflamed the continual wars of the Seventeenth Century, which were usually fought for commercial advantages. English privateers were unleashed on the maritime trade of national rivals, and Parliament was ruthless in its suppression of independent commerce by its American colonies. The Navigation Act sought to keep all mercantile activities within the British Empire and prohibited the colonies from trading directly with other countries.

The Enlightenment and Individual Rights

The enlightened thinkers of the age began to reflect upon how Parliament was controlled by land owners and business interests and to consider the manner in which towns and villages were ably governed by elders and guild councils. They concluded that even commoners might possess some inherent rights in self-government, and ultimately, perhaps it was the people themselves who were sovereign. The idea was expanded to include the right of all people to shape their own lives as best they could, without interference from church or state.

Among the hundreds of leading intellectuals of the Age of Enlightenment, five can be singled out as having the greatest influence on the development of American republicanism:

Francis Bacon (1561-1626) was an attorney, scientist and philosopher. He studied several European governments, before becoming the Attorney General of England and proposed the essential elements of English Common Law. A political reformer, Bacon wrote a novel about a utopia in the Pacific Ocean, in which there was freedom of religion and political expression. He helped establish the English colonies in the Americas and was highly influential in their charters, which allowed limited self-government. Reason, for Bacon, was paramount, and he urged others to seek truth no matter where it leads irrespective of any offense it might bring. He believed, "the sovereignty of Man lieth hid in knowledge . . . which kings with their treasure cannot buy, nor with their force command."

Thomas Hobbes (1588-1679), an English philosopher, first wrote about the social contract in a civil society between the people of a state and the legitimacy of its government. He believed the people themselves possessed the sovereign power, which they shared with their government for the protection it afforded. A government that failed in its duties to provide welfare, protection and justice must be dissolved and replaced by another commonwealth.

John Locke (1632-1704), an English physician and philosopher, believed reason and tolerance were inherent in human nature, as our brains are like a blank slate at birth. Most important was the manner in which individuals are educated. He elaborated on the necessity of individual consent for the political legitimacy of representative government, and he advocated the right to defend one's "Life, health, Liberty, or

Possessions." For Locke, the "careful and constant pursuit of true and solid happiness" was the greatest good.

Adam Smith (1723-1790), a Scottish philosopher, expressed his thoughts on political economic theory and mercantilism in the *Wealth of Nations*. Smith believed self-interest and competition formed an "invisible hand" to promote economic prosperity for society as a whole. At the same time, he repeatedly warned against cabals and monopolies, which interfered with free enterprise and harmed society.

Immanuel Kant (1724-1804), a German philosopher, believed in a "representative republic," in which no citizen would be bound by any law of government he did not consent to. He said, "this idea obliges every legislator to pass laws in such a way that they would have been able to arise from the united will of an entire people and to regard every subject, insofar as he wishes to be a citizen, as though he had given his assent to this will. For that is the touchstone of the lawfulness of any public law." Kant's credo was "dare to think for yourself."

Such ideas were intended to illuminate, and the ability of these writers to circulate and project their thinking was made possible by the prevailing freedom of the press. While France employed censors to review publications, England enjoyed a free market of published ideas. Thousands of books and millions of pamphlets were printed, while dozens of newspapers circulated. The press had been free of licensing since 1695, and copyright laws protected publishers and authors. Rapid communication was aided by as many as six daily postal deliveries in London and major cities. Reading became commonplace, and far more ordinary people knew how to read, than to write.

Many of the earlier wars that swept Europe were fueled by religious passion, rather than economic interests. Over time, nation states supporting different religions began to unite in economic warfare, and religious toleration became more widespread.

As intellectuals considered the Judeo-Christian religions and compared them to those of Islam, India and China, many began to look to the God revealed by universal reason as the best guide to morality and virtue. These Deists believed natural religion was complete, and Judaism, Christianity and other revealed religions were mere superstitions. Deists believed rational people could find God for themselves. Rather than argue against the established religions, the Deists were tolerant of all and supported the right of everyone to make up their own mind.

More than just freedom of religion and speech, an evolving concept of political liberty lent itself to rational analysis during the English Enlightenment. If, as Locke believed, everyone is born with a clean slate for a mind, then everyone starts out equal. All people have natural rights over the product of their own thinking and efforts. These rights extended to equality before the law and its equal protection, freedom to be secure in one's own home and property, freedom from absolute government and arbitrary arrest, and freedom to participate in one's own government through elections.

As the Eighteenth Century reached its midpoint in England, those who asserted the universality of liberty looked upon the infringement and repression of individual rights by the government and corporate interests, and decided something could and should be done. Some relied on fiction and novels to express and cloak their dissatisfaction, while others called outright for a formal expression of individual rights.

The Society of the Supporters of the Bill of Rights proposed that all parliamentary candidates be required to take a position on "full and equal representation of the people in parliament, annual elections, redress of grievances before granting supplies, bans on pensions and places, attention to the Irish problem and restoration to America of the 'essential right of taxation.'"

Belief in the "Rights of Englishmen" was shared by the American colonists, who were reading the same books, pamphlets and newspapers as their contemporaries in England. At least two-thirds of men in the American colonies were literate, and they had a large appetite for the written product of the Enlightenment. Coming to believe their rights were being infringed upon by the English government, these men decided to do something about it. While the American colonists built upon the political and philosophical foundation they inherited from England, the edifice of government they constructed was unlike anything ever seen before.

CREATION OF A REPUBLIC

In what many historians have called the first world war, England fought alongside Portugal, Prussia and the smaller German states against France, Spain, Austria and Sweden in the Seven Years' War. Deploying the greatest land army, Prussia primarily waged the war in Europe. England defended the oceans with its large navy and fought overseas against France and its native allies in North America, where the conflict was known as the French and Indian War.

The war ended in 1763 with an English-Prussian victory, and the win extended the domination of England in North America to the Mississippi River. The war had cost both sides more than a million lives, and it left England with a national debt of £132 million.

As the Exchequer (England's treasury) searched for ways to balance its books, it looked westward to the American colonies. Receiving their charters from the Crown, the colonies had been founded as corporate arms of the British Empire to produce a profit, and their defense had contributed to a good portion of the war debt.

From the founding of Virginia in 1610 by the Virginia Company, and Massachusetts in 1628 by the Massachusetts Bay Company, a total of 13 colonies had received corporate charters from the Crown. King George I said it was upon commerce that "the riches and grandeur of this nation chiefly depend."

The English crown colonies were governed by legislators elected by the colonists and governors appointed by the king. The colonies were designed to be self-sufficient and were empowered to pass their own regulatory laws, including the collection of taxes and import duties, subject only to the governor's veto. Operating a large fleet of indigenously constructed ships, the colonists were notorious smugglers, who sought to avoid imperial trading restrictions and the payment of duties.

Taxation Without Representation

Parliament passed a tax on colonial sugar in 1764 and the Stamp Act in 1765. A direct tax was to be collected on every single piece of printed paper used in the colonies, including legal documents, bills of sale, newspapers, and even playing cards, by forcing them to bear stamps. The colonists were outraged! Unlike their own legislatures, the people had not voted for the members of Parliament who levied the tax on them.

The outcry was "Taxation without representation is tyranny!" It was published and republished up and down the colonial coastline; boycotts of English goods were organized and riots took place in the major cities. The Stamp Act was repealed by Parliament; however, its members began to take a harder look at their American creation. Holding that the colonists had "virtual representation," Parliament passed the Declaratory Act in 1766 proclaiming its right to tax the colonists.

Parliament followed up the next year with the Townshend Acts, named after the Chancellor of the Exchequer. One intention of the Acts was to raise money in the colonies for the government to pay the salaries of colonial judges and governors, instead of having them directly paid by the colonies. This was done to secure the officials' loyalty to the British government and to ensure reliable rulings on imperial trade regulations. Another purpose of the acts was to force the colonists to pay for maintaining the English Army in America.

The tax was on the import of tea, paper, glass, lead, and paint, which the colonists could only buy from England. Enforcement of the tax was aided by general search warrants, which allowed customs officials to easily seize smuggled and untaxed goods.

Massachusetts, Virginia and Pennsylvania sent protest petitions to Parliament—which were ignored. Boycotts were organized, including one in Virginia by George Washington. The Acts provided for an American Customs Board in Boston, which began to strictly enforce the Acts. When Bostonians protested, the Board requested military protection. A fifty-gun warship entered the harbor in May 1768, and four regiments of the British Army arrived in October.

Civil unrest ensued after a Boston youth was killed by a customs employee in March 1770. A crowd of Bostonians surrounded an army sentry and began to harass him and other troops who came to his assistance. The soldiers fired their rifles into the crowd, killing five and wounding others, in the Boston Massacre. The soldiers were brought to trial and were defended by attorney John Adams. Six were acquitted, and two were convicted of manslaughter and were branded on their hands.

Coincidentally, on the same day as the Massacre, Parliament rescinded portions of the Townshend Acts, except for the levy on tea.

Traditionally, the salaries of the governor and judges in Massachusetts had been paid by its colonial legislature; however, beginning in 1772, they were to be paid from the collection of custom duties. The change reduced local authority, and the legislature asked John Adams to write an objection. He argued the colony's original charter was signed by the king, and the colony's allegiance was to the Crown, and not to Parliament. Adams concluded that Parliament had no authority over the colony and, unless that fact was acknowledged, the colony would be forced to declare independence.

The East India Company shipped tea from India and China to supply the English (and colonial) caffeine addiction; however, an immense overstock of tea and the outflow of silver required to pay for the product was threatening both the corporate and the government balance sheets. In 1773, as a specific benefit, Parliament exempted the corporation from certain import duties into England, as long as the tea was directly shipped on to the colonies. The fact that many members of the British government and royal family were stockholders in the East India Company undoubtedly aided in passage of the law.

The colonists were appalled by the corporate favoritism. While they might individually pay less for their cup of tea, the Act undercut the prices of American merchants and threatened to put them out of business.

East India Company ships carrying untaxed tea were turned away in Philadelphia and New York, and the tea cargo was seized in Charleston. When the corporate ships arrived in Boston, they were boarded during the night by colonists disguised as Indians. More than 90,000 pounds of tea, valued at £9,659 ($1.7 million today), were dumped into the harbor, in the Boston Tea Party.

John Adams wrote, "This destruction of the Tea is so bold, so daring, so firm, intrepid and inflexible, and it must have so important Consequences, and so lasting, that I can't but consider it as an Epoch in History."

It was Parliament's turn to be outraged. It passed the Coercive Acts in early 1774, which closed Boston's harbor until the destroyed tea was paid for. Moreover, Parliament unilaterally changed the Massachusetts charter, requiring its legislators to be appointed by London. Town meetings without consent were prohibited, and more troops were dispatched to Boston, some of whom were quartered in private homes. If the members of Parliament thought they could coerce the colonists to fall into line, they were gravely mistaken.

Thomas Jefferson, a Virginian trained in the law, wrote *A Summary View of the Rights of British America* in 1774. In the tract, Jefferson denounced British coercion, repudiated Parliament's right to impose taxes on the colonies and listed the grievances against King George III and the English government. Jefferson believed in the leadership of enlightened individuals, who had the duty to guard "the sacred deposit of the rights and liberties of their fellow citizens."

The Continental Congresses

In response to the "Intolerable Acts," the American colonies (except Georgia) sent 55 delegates, including John Adams, to a Continental Congress. Thomas Jefferson was not a delegate; however, his *Summary View* was widely discussed.

The meeting of the Congress in Philadelphia during September 1774 resulted in a Continental Association, which called for a boycott of English goods—unless Parliament rescinded the Acts. The Congress proclaimed that only colonial legislatures could lay taxes on the colonists, subject to a Royal veto. The Association requested locally organized Committees of Safety to regulate prices and enforce the boycott.

The Continental Congress issued a Petition to the "King's Most Excellent Majesty," which included a long list of grievances, recounted the colonies' birth as "the heirs of freedom," and reaffirmed their "strongest love of liberty." Asking "but for Peace, Liberty and Safety," the "faithful People in America" beseeched that "your Royal authority and interposition may be used for our relief, ..." In a single word—the members demanded "Liberty."

His Royal Majesty, King George III did not provide relief to his loyal subjects in America, and the people of Massachusetts resolved to resist the Parliamentary appointment of its legislative representatives. A shadow colonial government was organized, with an independent legislature, and local militias were formed, armed and trained. In February 1775, Parliament declared Massachusetts to be in a State of Rebellion.

When the British Army marched out of Boston to confiscate weapons and gunpowder on April 19, 1775, the people's militias of Lexington and Concord defended their communities and colonial government. They fired the "shot heard round the world." The British Army retreated, under sustained gunfire and heavy losses, to Charlestown and Boston, where they were besieged by rebel forces.

A Second Continental Congress convened in the summer of 1775, with John Adams once again in attendance. He was joined by Thomas Jefferson and George Washington, who had distinguished himself in the French and Indian War as commander of the Virginia forces, and by Benjamin Franklin of Philadelphia, an eminent scientific philosopher and publisher.

The primary task of the Congress was to take control of the Revolutionary War, which had commenced in a haphazard manner. John Adams' nomination of George Washington to be commander-in-chief of the Continental Army was approved, and Washington left to take command of the rebel army in Boston.

The Congress prepared a Declaration of Causes for the conflict and made another attempt to compromise, sending a minister to negotiate with the English government. Taking on all aspects of governing, except raising taxes, the Congress set about to print paper money, borrow hard currency in Europe, and to raise and equip an army.

The Declaration of Independence and the Articles of Confederacy

Remaining constantly in session, the Congress passed a resolution in May 1776 calling on all colonies to form revolutionary governments to support independence. In a radical preamble written by John Adams, colonies were urged to disavow oaths of allegiance to the Crown and to suppress English authority.

Believing it necessary to engage in relations with foreign nations, the Congress resolved the need for a declaration of independence. Separate committees were formed to draft the declaration, a model treaty with other nations, and Articles of Confederation.

Benjamin Franklin, John Adams, and Thomas Jefferson were appointed to the declaration committee, with Jefferson primarily responsible for writing a first draft. After minor changes by the other members, the draft was submitted to the Congress. Among the charges Jefferson made against the King was the imposition of slavery. Jefferson condemned slavery as an "assemblage of horrors" that violated "sacred [natural] rights." In editing down Jefferson's original draft by one-third, Congress deleted his attack on slavery.

Adams carried the debate in the Congress, resulting in an edited and approved version being signed by the delegates on July 4, 1776. The second paragraph of the declaration expresses the years of enlightened thinking that culminated in the document:

> We hold these truths to be self-evident, that all men are created equal, that they are endowed by their Creator with certain unalienable Rights, that among these are Life, Liberty and the pursuit of Happiness. That to secure these rights, Governments are instituted among Men, deriving their just powers from the consent of the governed. That whenever any Form of Government becomes destructive of these ends, it is the Right of the People to alter or to abolish it, and to institute new Government, laying its foundation on such principles and organizing its powers in such form, as to them shall seem most likely to effect their Safety and Happiness.

Following a year of debate, the Articles of Confederation were submitted to the colonies for ratification on November 15, 1777; however, it took more than three years for all to agree. Virginia was the first and Maryland was the last—on March 1, 1781. The Congress of the Confederation met the next day for the first time.

Each of the United States had one vote in the new Congress, which did not have the power to raise troops or directly levy taxes to support the war effort. These two factors were to be the primary limitations of the confederation government and imposed the greatest burden on Washington's fighting of a war without adequate manpower or supplies.

Under Washington's command, the Continental Army fairly quickly forced the British Army to evacuate Boston; however, Washington thereafter suffered a series of defeats that almost ended the Revolution. Rallying the soldiers and the new nation at its darkest hour were the writings of an immigrant teacher. In *Common Sense*, Thomas Paine wrote, plainly, to ordinary people about having "a government of our own" and the "power to begin the world over again."

On December 23, 1776, after almost two years of defeats and just as the enlistments of more than a fifth of his soldiers were to expire, General Washington ordered these words written by Paine in *The American Crisis* to be read aloud to all of his troops:

> These are the times that try men's souls. The summer soldier and the sunshine patriot will, in this crisis, shrink from the service of their country; but he that stands it now, deserves the love and thanks of man and woman. Tyranny, like hell, is not easily conquered; yet we have this consolation with us, that the harder the conflict, the more glorious the triumph. What we obtain too cheap, we esteem too lightly; it is dearness only that gives everything its value.

With its Declaration of Independence, the United States began to receive military supplies and financial assistance from France, Spain and the Dutch Republic. France and Spain formally allied themselves with the United States and were instrumental in the defeat of the English Navy at the Battle of the Chesapeake in

September 1781 and the British Army at Yorktown, Virginia the following month. Among the officers leading the assault on English fortifications at Yorktown was Colonel Alexander Hamilton of New York, who had distinguished himself throughout the War as Washington's chief of staff.

Also fighting at Yorktown was the First Regiment of Rhode Island, made up of former slaves who earned their freedom by enlisting. The black soldiers were veterans of numerous battles, and the Regiment was considered to be "the most neatly dressed, the best under arms, and the most precise in its maneuvers."

With little actual fighting taking place, the Revolutionary War technically continued for another two years, until it was ended by the Treaty of Paris in 1783.

The Constitution of the United States of America

Having won the revolution, the leaders of the new nation had to administer its independence. United in the war, they were divided on how to implement the peace. A paramount concern was the weakness of the Articles of Confederation, which had hampered the Congress in conducting the war and threatened the ability of the government to administer statehood. The Confederation had been formed by the states and not by the people, thus depriving it of popular support.

The executive power was very weak, being exercised by the president of the Congress. Legislators were elected annually, and a vote of nine of the thirteen states was required for all significant legislation. Tax measures required unanimous consent. Matters of national importance, such as trade and revenue, were left up to the individual states. Any attempt to amend the Articles required the unanimous consent of all states.

The economy was depressed—there was a shortage of hard money in circulation, and debts weighed heavily on farmers and workers. Minor rebellions took place in Vermont, Virginia, and New York. In early 1787, two thousand poor and hungry farmers, many of them veterans, marched on the Springfield arsenal in Massachusetts. They were confronted by the militia and many were killed.

State legislators, most of whom were elected annually, responded to the demands of their impoverished constituents with legislation providing debt relief, often to the dismay of creditors. Politicians sympathetic to financial interests decried this "excess of democracy" or "democratical tyranny." Democracy was interfering with the ability of money lenders to collect debts, and they resented its free exercise.

Leaders throughout the states realized that changes had to be made in the Articles of Confederation. Writing to Thomas Jefferson, who was serving as minister in France, Washington said, "That something is necessary, all will agree; for the situation of the general Government (if it can be called a government) is shaken to its foundation . . . . In a word, it is at an end, and unless a remedy is soon applied, anarchy & confusion will inevitably ensue."

A convention to consider the problems was organized in Philadelphia in May 1787. George Washington presided over the convention, and Alexander Hamilton, his former aide, and James Madison, his fellow Virginian, played leading roles. Fairly quickly, the decision was made to create a new government, rather than reform the old one.

Meeting in great secrecy, the convention began its deliberations with the Virginia Plan, an initial draft proposal written by Madison and approved by Washington. The members also considered the constitutions of the various states, and John Adams' recently published *Defence of the Constitutions of the United States of America* and earlier *Thoughts on Government* were highly influential.

Primary issues included the manner in which the president, vice president and senators were to be elected, the allocation of House representatives by population, and finally whether slaves should be counted in the apportionment. A compromise allowing slaves to count as three-fifths of a "person" carried the day, and the Virginia Plan was largely adopted. Fearing the ability of one person to start wars, the power to declare war was vested in the multiple members of congress.

The proposed constitution created a republic, in which power was balanced between a strong executive, a congress consisting of a senate and house of representatives, and an independent judiciary. The Constitution was signed by members of the convention on September 17, 1787 and submitted to the states for ratification.

As a brilliant reflection of the Enlightenment, the Constitution was a contract between the People and their government:

> We the People of the United States, in Order to form a more perfect Union, establish Justice, insure domestic Tranquility, provide for the common defense, promote the general Welfare and secure the Blessings of Liberty to ourselves and our Posterity, do ordain and establish this Constitution for the United States of America.

Immediately, differences of opinion led to factions. The Federalists, led by Hamilton, strongly supported a strong central federal government as provided for in the Constitution. The Anti-Federalists, led by Madison and Jefferson, primarily objected to excessive executive power and the absence of an individual bill of rights.

Principally written by Hamilton and Madison between October 1787 and August 1788, *The Federalist Papers* consisted of 85 essays promoting ratification of the Constitution by the states. Collectively, the essays helped to define the meaning and intent of the Constitution. Passionately written and intellectually brilliant, the *Papers* carried the day, and the Constitution became operative after it was approved by the first nine states within ten months of its submission.

The new government came into existence on March 4, 1789, and the remainder of the states ratified the Constitution by the following year. George Washington received more than two-thirds of the Electoral College votes and was elected President. John Adams received the second largest number of votes and was elected Vice President.

Introduced by newly-elected Representative James Madison of Virginia, the Congress of the United States proposed the first 10 amendments to the Constitution as a Bill of Rights on September 25, 1789. The amendments were ratified by the states in 1791. The Bill of Rights balanced the individual rights of the governed with the power of the government established by their consent.

The essence of the representative government created by the Constitution was that the republic was responsible to the People generally, but it also protected private minority business and financial interests from a public majority exercising an "excess of democracy." The government institutions resulting from the Constitution were designed to guarantee both liberty and order.

The government represented the People, but in an indirect way. The president was elected by the Electoral College, and U.S. senators and most public officers in the states were selected or appointed by the state legislatures, rather than by direct elections.

The manner of voting and qualifications of voters were left up to individual states to define. The right to vote was neither included in the Constitution, nor in the Bill of Rights. That omission has never been corrected.

When asked what kind of government had been formed by the Constitutional Convention, Benjamin Franklin replied, "A Republic, if you can keep it."

The Growth of Freedom

As the new government assembled in New York City, there were differences about the direction it would take, but all were in agreement about who would lead. George Washington was not only a Revolutionary War hero, he was also the richest man in America.

Magisterially conveyed across the Hudson in a large barge rowed by sailors in white uniforms, Washington entered the city—where many expected him to become king of the new nation. There were debates about whether he should be called "His Elective Majesty" or "His Mightiness." He quickly discounted the idea of a dynasty, letting it be known that he "had no family to build in greatness upon my Country's ruin."

In his brief inaugural address, Washington prophesized:

> When the people shall find themselves secure under an energetic government, when foreign Nations shall be disposed to give us equal advantages in commerce from dread of retaliation, when the burdens of the war shall be in a manner done away by the sale of western lands, when the seeds of happiness which are sown here shall begin to expand themselves, and when everyone (under his own vine and fig-tree) shall begin to taste the fruits of freedom—then all these

blessings (for all these blessings will come) will be referred to the fostering influence of the new government.

Forming a Government

Washington surrounded himself with the best of the minds that had created the republic: Vice President John Adams, who presided over the Senate; Congressman James Madison, who not only drafted the congressional welcome of Washington, but helped write Washington's response in his inaugural address; Thomas Jefferson, who served as Secretary of State and managed foreign affairs; and Alexander Hamilton, who served as Secretary of the Treasury and took on the task of balancing the nation's financial accounts.

As the ship of state sailed into uncharted waters, many rocks, shoals and reefs had been left unmapped by the Constitution and the Federalist Papers. Obstacles included formation of the judiciary system, how to handle the national debt, and what to do about slavery.

With the passage of the Judiciary Act of 1789, Washington appointed John Jay as the first Chief Justice. Jay had served as President of the Continental Congress, negotiated the Treaty of Paris, and contributed to the Federalist Papers. As Chief Justice, Jay established the Judicial Branch of government and institutionalized Washington's commitment to an independent judiciary.

An audit of the Confederation's financial records revealed the United States had inherited a national debt of $77 million owed to its citizens, the states, and foreign nations. It took Alexander Hamilton three months to wade through the red ink, before recommending that all debts be consolidated, including those owed by the states for war expenses.

Perhaps the most competent of Washington's cabinet members, Hamilton not only formulated the new government's economic policy, he created the power of the federal government to implement the policy.

Hamilton proposed all debts be paid at par value and a National Bank be created to manage revenues, investments and the payment of debts. Virginia had already paid most of its debt and loudly objected to having to assume the debts of other states. Murmuring secession, Virginia and its Congressional delegation, including James Madison, objected to Hamilton's plan. Washington remained above the fray, allowing the factions to work out a solution. Following a fierce debate, Congress passed legislation supporting Hamilton's program and sent it to Washington for signature.

Washington received written objections from Jefferson and Madison, who, along with the Attorney General, argued the Constitution provided no power to create corporations, such as a national bank, and that under the Tenth Amendment, all powers not granted to the federal government, were reserved to the states.

Washington sent the arguments to Hamilton for comment. In a 13,000-word rebuttal, Hamilton relied on the "necessary and proper" clause of the Constitution, wherein implied powers were granted to the federal government. With the political cover provided by Hamilton's brief, Washington signed the legislation he wanted.

Hamilton submitted a *Report on Manufactures* to Congress in 1791, which recognized the procurement of "all such machines as are known in any part of Europe can only require a proper provision and due pains." Inasmuch as the export of machines used to produce textiles and the emigration of people trained in their construction and operation were felony crimes in England, the *Report* became the basis for the United States to illicitly obtain European manufacturing technologies and the immigration of technicians to assemble and operate them.

The unresolved issue of slavery came before Congress in the form of Quaker petitions to immediately end the slavery trade and to gradually abolish slavery. Since the final petition was signed by Benjamin Franklin, Congress was forced to debate the issues. Washington shared Franklin's views on gradual emancipation, but he quietly supported Madison's position that the matter be tabled until 1808, prior to which time the Constitution did not allow legislation on the migration or importation of slaves.

When the government relocated to Philadelphia, Washington was concerned his household slaves, who accompanied him, could demand emancipation after six months, as allowed by Pennsylvania state law. His cook, Hercules, did not petition for his freedom, but, rather than return to Virginia, he disappeared when Washington's second term expired. In his last will and testament, Washington freed all of his slaves.

The debate over a permanent national capital continued in Congress, with James Madison, quietly supported by Washington, arguing for a location on the Potomac—the geographic center of the 13 states. Over a dinner in Jefferson's apartment, and after a few bottles of wine, a secret deal was reached in which Hamilton guaranteed enough northern votes for the Potomac site—if Madison and his southern coalition would support Hamilton's program for assuming the national debt. At Jefferson's suggestion, Washington undertook the executive responsibility for locating and planning the District of Columbia.

Washington's plans for the Federal City took shape during and after his terms in office. What has never been realized was his dream of a national university in the city to bring together the brightest minds of the nation to study and share the common experience of living in a free and democratic country.

As France's own brand of revolution swept that country and rekindled its war with England, Washington administered a restrained foreign policy that maintained neutrality and avoided war. He primarily looked westward to consolidate the territory of the United States to the Mississippi River and sought to make peace with its native inhabitants. He considered the Indian tribes to be foreign nations—rather than the citizens of any state—and sought to recognize their sovereign "homelands."

The Emergence of Political Parties

Individual members of Congress had different philosophies and points of view, but most were highly principled. Their debates were spirited; however, they generally respected the character and opinions of others. Most worked for intelligent compromises which best served the People of the new nation.

With the success of Hamilton's assumption of debt, the imposition of a protective tariff and the continuing irresolution of the slavery issue, the South feared the rising power of northern commerce and industry encouraged by Hamilton and the Federalist Party. In opposition, the group led by Jefferson and Madison began to consolidate into the Democratic-Republican Party, which arose from a society by the same name that was hostile to a monarchical presidency.

There would be future realignments, reorganizations and renaming; however, the two-party system became firmly entrenched in American politics. The Democratic-Republican Party was commonly called the Republican Party, although it is not related to either of the current parties by the same names. In political science, this period in which the Federalist and Republican Parties prevailed is known as the "First Party System."

While Jefferson and Hamilton came to personally despise each other, and Jefferson agitated against administration policy, they continued to work together in the administration, and Washington relied on the advice and counsel of both.

Hamilton resigned from the cabinet prior to the end of Washington's second term, but he retained a high degree of influence and wrote Washington's Farewell Address. Washington did a final edit of the Address and submitted it for publication, never actually giving it as a speech. The Address directly challenged the Republican threat:

> This government, . . . has first claim to your confidence and support . . . . The very idea of the power and right of the People to establish Government presupposes the duty of every Individual to obey the established government.

The presidential election to succeed Washington pitted John Adams and the Federalists against Thomas Jefferson and the Republicans. Under the political traditions of the time, neither admitted they were candidates.

Adams and Jefferson had cooperated on writing the Declaration of Independence and as ministers to England and France during the Revolutionary War. They began to rub on one another after Adams received the most votes for Vice President, and as they both served in the Washington administration. With the hardening of lines between Federalists and Republicans, the distance between the two men increased, especially as anonymous essays began to appear in partisan publications highlighting their differences and attacking their positions.

John Adams and the Federalists

In the election of 1796, the Federalists accused the Republicans of supporting the violence of the French Revolution, and the Republicans accused the Federalists of favoring the aristocracy and monarchies. John Adams received 71 electoral votes and Thomas Jefferson received 68, making him the Vice President in the Adams administration.

With the Twelfth Amendment in 1803 changing the manner in which Presidents and Vice Presidents are elected, the 1796 election was the first and only time the two offices were filled by candidates from opposing parties.

Adam's single-term presidential administration was conservative; he retained the cabinet he inherited from Washington, which Hamilton continued to manipulate in the background; he began to buildup the Navy, to defend the United States against threats of war from France; and he signed the Alien and Sedition Acts of 1798, which punished "false, scandalous, and malicious" writings against the government. Adams believed that the government should led by "the rich, the well born, and the able."

In opposition to the Acts, Jefferson secretly drafted the Kentucky Resolutions, which proclaimed the "natural right" of each state to nullify unconstitutional federal laws and actions. While failing to provide full support to Adams, Jefferson did not overtly undercut the administration in Congress, where he served as President of the Senate. Consistent with his character, Jefferson wrote a manual of parliamentary rules for the Senate, which continues in effect to this day.

In 1800, following the death of Washington, the government moved to the District of Columbia, and the Federal City was named for the "Father of the Country." Adams occupied the White House and offered this benediction: "I pray heaven to bestow the best of blessing on this house and all that shall hereafter inhabit. May none but honest and wise men ever rule under this roof."

In a speech opening the Capitol, Adams said:

May this territory be the residence of virtue and happiness! In this city may that piety and virtue, that wisdom and magnanimity, that constancy and self-government, which adorned the great character whose name it bears, be forever held in veneration!

One of the most significant actions taken by Adams during his presidency was the last-minute nomination of John Marshall, his Secretary of State, to be Chief Justice of the Supreme Court. Marshall would dominate the Court for the next 34 years and was responsible for creating the power of the Court to serve as an effective balance to the Legislative and Executive Branches of government. Marshall conceived the priority of judicial review of both state and federal laws for compliance with the Constitution, and he promoted the rule of law throughout the new nation.

In the election of 1800, Adams suffered from the unpopularity of the Alien and Sedition Acts—which he admitted was the greatest blunder of his presidency—and a nasty personal attack by fellow Federalist Alexander Hamilton.

Jefferson made a political deal with Aaron Burr, which provided New York's electoral votes to Jefferson and the Vice Presidency for Burr. In an ironic twist, the two tied for votes in the Electoral College—Burr refused to concede, and the election had to be decided by the House of Representatives. After the thirty-sixth ballot, one Federalist representative changed his vote, allowing Thomas Jefferson to become President. John Adams graciously gave his good wishes to Jefferson.

Thomas Jefferson, the Virginia Dynasty, and the First Republican Party

President Jefferson sought to interject a note of compromise and reason in his inaugural address:

> We are all Republicans, we are all Federalists. If there be any among us who wish to dissolve this Union or to change its republican form, let them stand undisturbed as monuments of the safety with which error of opinion may be tolerated where reason is left free to combat it.

Although it was the Federalists who primarily believed in a strong executive, Jefferson, with the able assistance of his Secretary of State, James Madison, set about to make full use of the powers he inherited and to expand them in unforeseen ways.

Of immediate concern was the western territory known as Louisiana, which had just come under the domination of France and its emperor, Napoléon Bonaparte. The area west of the Mississippi River, from the Gulf of Mexico to Canada, and west to Oregon consisted of 828,000 square miles of virgin wilderness. Jefferson and Madison dispatched another Virginian,

James Monroe, to negotiate American shipping rights down the Mississippi River through New Orleans.

Napoléon, who had suffered great losses in his attempts to quell a slave rebellion in Saint-Domingue (Haiti) and facing another war with England, was ready to make a deal. Threatening an alliance with England in the alternative, Monroe negotiated the purchase of the entire territory of Louisiana for $15 million, or about four cents per acre. The purchase instantly doubled the size of the United States, and although there were questions about the constitutionality of the purchase, the common law expression that "possession is nine-tenths of the law" prevailed, and the Senate ratified the purchase treaty.

Jefferson remained concerned about corporate influence in the government, saying "I hope we shall crush in its birth the aristocracy of our moneyed corporations which dare already to challenge our government to a trial by strength, and bid defiance to the laws of our country." He feared "the selfish spirit of commerce [that] knows no country, and feels no passion or principle but that of gain." Jefferson, through his correspondence with James Madison, attempted and failed to have the "freedom of commerce against monopolies" included in the Bill of Rights.

Although Jefferson's Declaration of Independence spoke of the equality of man, none of the states prohibited slavery, and there was little equality provided by the state laws regulating voting. Virtually all states required voters to own property, although Pennsylvania, New Hampshire, Delaware, Georgia and North Carolina began to allow all taxpayers to vote. Vermont allowed all men to vote, and for a time, Tennessee provided universal male suffrage, including free blacks. Only New Jersey allowed the possibility of female suffrage; however, it was later revoked.

The founders of the Constitution, especially Adams and Madison, did not believe in universal suffrage. Existing to this day, the manner in which voting takes place, including written, rather than voice, balloting, was left up to the states to decide and has never been changed. The states are not even required to hold presidential elections—they retain the constitutional option to appoint Electors by legislative vote.

Throughout his presidency, Jefferson aggressively seized land from native American tribes, up to 200,000 square miles, and he encouraged white settlements throughout the areas once declared by George Washington to be sovereign homelands. He threatened any tribe that attacked white settlers that he would drive them across the Mississippi as the only condition of peace.

Following his retirement, Jefferson and John Adams resolved their differences and carried on a cordial correspondence for many years. On his deathbed in Massachusetts in the evening of July 4, 1826, John Adams final words were, "Thomas Jefferson survives"—which was not true. Jefferson had died earlier in the afternoon, on the anniversary of the Declaration of Independence they had written 50 years before.

Unlike Washington, Thomas Jefferson was heavily in debt and did not generally emancipate his slaves in his will. Jefferson had earlier allowed a son and daughter, whom he had fathered with Sally Hemings, his slave and longtime concubine, to leave his plantation and to live as free whites. Jefferson did legally emancipate his other two slave sons by Sally Hemings in his will; however, he did not release their mother. Sally Hemings was inherited by Jefferson's daughter. Hemings was later "given her time," an unofficial freedom, which allowed her to live in Virginia with her freed sons until her death.

Jefferson was followed into office by James Madison, who shared Jefferson's fear of corporate power:

> There is an evil which ought to be guarded against in the indefinite accumulation of property from the capacity of holding it in perpetuity by . . . corporations. The power of all corporations ought to be limited in this respect. The growing wealth acquired by them never fails to be a source of abuses.

Madison was succeeded by James Monroe, another member of the Virginia Dynasty that governed the nation for 24 years. Other than for the brief War of 1812, which saw the English chasing Madison out of Washington, DC and burning the White House and Capitol, it was mostly a time of peace and expansion. The slavery issue remained unresolved and continued to be an issue in the settlement and governing of the western territories.

The Unique Presidency of John Quincy Adams

Having served all of the previous presidents, including Washington and his own father, John Quincy Adams was possibly the most qualified presidential candidate of all times. He was fluent in Latin, Greek, French, Dutch, German and other European languages. As a young man, Adams helped negotiate recognition of the United States by Russia, and he was minister to the Netherlands, Portugal and Prussia. Breaking with the Federalists, he served in the U.S. Senate, before becoming Madison's ambassador to Russia. Adams was recalled to negotiate the end of the War of 1812 and was appointed as Madison's ambassador to England.

James Monroe appointed Adams as his Secretary of State. Adams negotiated the treaties which acquired Florida for the United States and defined the border between the western United States and Canada. Adams wrote the Monroe Doctrine. It held that any attempt by European powers to colonize or interfere with any American country would be considered an act of aggression. Not only did the Doctrine help curtail United States' own ambitions as an imperial power, it allowed the South and Central American nations to develop and maintain their independence.

By the presidential election of 1824, the original Federalist Party was no longer viable, and the Republican Party was on the verge of extinction. By a variety of *ad hoc* measures, three presidential candidates emerged: Andrew Jackson from Tennessee, John Quincy Adams from Massachusetts, and House Speaker Henry Clay from Kentucky.

Even though Jackson won almost as many popular votes as Clay and Adams combined, he failed to obtain the required majority in the Electoral College. Acting pursuant to the Twelfth Amendment, the House of Representatives decided for Adams on the first ballot.

Adams appointed Henry Clay, who had yielded his electoral votes to Adams, as his Secretary of State. Since this was the cabinet position earlier held by the previous three presidents, the Jacksonians claimed a "corrupt bargain" had been struck for Clay to succeed Adams. The extreme hostility of the Jacksonian "Democrats," and their gaining control of Congress in the mid-term elections of 1826, doomed Adams to the same one-term presidency as his father.

Following his presidency, John Quincy Adams was elected to serve the people of Massachusetts in the House of

Representatives. In 1841, Adams defended a group of African slaves who had been kidnapped in Sierra Leone and illegally transported in a Spanish ship (*La Amistad*) to Cuba. The Africans managed to kill the captain and take control of the ship, before it was seized off the coast of New York by the U.S. Navy.

The question of whether the men and women should be returned to Cuba, repatriated to Africa, or freed was decided in Federal Court proceedings and appealed to the Supreme Court. In obtaining their freedom, Adams argued the men and women were "entitled to all the provisions of the law of nations, and the protection and comfort which the laws of that State secure to every human being within its limits."

The Expansion of Democracy

By the presidential election in 1828, the United States had changed in many ways during the half century since its formation. There were 24 states—they had all adopted free white male suffrage, and elections were rambunctious. The new Democratic Party represented the farmers and artisans against the business and financial interests, who wanted a larger and more active government.

Andrew Jackson, who believed even the poorest white male should be allowed to vote, was the Democratic Party presidential candidate. President Adams was the candidate of the Republican Party. When Jackson was called a "jackass" in the opposition press, he adopted the donkey as the mascot of the Democratic Party. Three times as many white men voted in the election as did four years earlier, and most voted for Jackson. Following his landslide victory, Jackson invited the ordinary people who elected him to attend a raucous "people's inaugural" in the White House.

Jackson had great faith in the people:

> Never for a moment believe that the great body of the citizens of any State or States can deliberately intend to do wrong. They may, under the influence of temporary excitement or misguided opinions, commit mistakes; they may be misled for a time by the suggestions of self-interest; but in a community so enlightened and patriotic as the people of the United States, argument will soon make them sensible of their errors, and when convinced they will be ready to repair them.

At the same time, Jackson feared the power of corporations:

> Unless you become more watchful in your states and check the spirit of monopoly and thirst for exclusive privileges, you will in the end find that . . . the control over your dearest interests has passed into the hands of these corporations.

The Republican Party of Jefferson and John Quincy Adams ceased to exist after the election, and a new Whig Party, representing Northern and Midwest business interests, was organized to take its place. Politically and economically, the Whigs were more in alignment with earlier Federalists, while the new Democratic Party was more Jeffersonian and agrarian based. Political scientists consider this period to be the "Second Party System."

Jackson fought a series of genocidal Seminole Wars in Florida and was primarily responsible for forcing the Native Americans of the Cherokee, Muscogee, Chickasaw, Choctaw and Seminole nations to relocate from large areas of tribal homeland in the Southeast to west of the Mississippi River—primarily to the Territory of Oklahoma. Driven by the U.S. Army, one quarter of the 16,000 Cherokees died along the "Trail of Tears."

Native Americans were not considered to be U.S. citizens and were rarely given judicial standing to oppose their removal. When the U.S. Supreme Court ruled Georgia could not impose laws within the Cherokee Nation, Jackson said, "John Marshall has made his decision; now let him enforce it! . . . Build a fire under them [the Indians]. When it gets hot enough, they'll go."

It was a time of massive immigration—the population exploded from 5.3 million in 1800 to 13 million in 1830—and internal migration to the West. As settlers put down roots, they formed local governments and public schools and governed themselves. As their numbers grew, they organized their territories into states. By the time Jackson left office after eight years, Arkansas, Michigan and Florida had joined the Union.

Replacing legislative appointments, most states began to allow direct election of state and county officials. It was at about this time the United States was visited by the French writer, Alexis de Tocqueville, who wrote *Democracy in America*. He observed:

In no country in the world does the law hold so absolute a language as in America; and in no country is the right of applying it vested in so many hands. The administrative power in the United States presents nothing either centralized or hierarchical in its constitution; this accounts for its passing unperceived. The power exists, but its representative is nowhere to be seen.

With homemade inventions, such as the cotton gin, and other industrial technology stolen from England and Europe, the United States began to turn out the tools and utensils needed by its expanding population. There was a growing middle class consisting of merchants, machinists, skilled craftsmen and professionals, and there were those who became wealthy from the labor of low-paid, unskilled workers supplied by the endless stream of immigrants.

A protective tariff was imposed on imported goods in support of domestic industry—primarily in the North. It resulted in higher prices having to be paid by other sectors, particularly the South, which remained agrarian.

John C. Calhoun, who had served as Vice President under both John Quincy Adams and Jackson, broke with Jackson after his first term. Calhoun became a U.S. Senator for South Carolina and supported state nullification of the protective tariff. A state convention declared that the tariffs were unconstitutional and unenforceable in South Carolina. Jackson prepared to use military force, but a compromise was reached. South Carolina repealed its Nullification Ordinance; however, a precedent for States' Rights was established—which would lead to civil war in just a few decades.

The Right of Secession

Virginia's original declaration ratifying the Constitution stated, "the powers granted under the Constitution being derived from the People of the United States may be resumed by them whensoever the same shall be perverted to their injury or oppression." Almost immediately, Virginia began to threaten secession over Alexander Hamilton's proposal to assume the debts of other states.

Among the founders, there was little doubt the states retained the right to leave the Republic. Writing in the Federalist Papers, James Madison said the Constitution would be ratified by the people, "not as individuals composing one entire nation, but as composing the distinct and independent states to which they respectively belong." He believed that, "The President derives his appointment from the States, and is periodically accountable to them."

Thomas Jefferson wrote the Kentucky Resolutions which held that the Constitution was a compact of the states, rather than a creation of the people as a whole. He said, "If there be any among us who would wish to dissolve this union, or to change its republican form, let them stand undisturbed as monuments of the safety with which error of opinion may be tolerated where reason is left to combat it."

The belief that individual states retained the right to secede was bipartisan. Upset by the ongoing War of 1812, the Federalists met in a secret constitutional convention at Hartford, Connecticut in 1815. Delegates considered secession by the New England states, including New York, and making a separate peace with England. Expulsion of the new western states from the Union was also considered. Writing the next year, Jefferson said, "If any state in the union will declare that it prefers separation . . . to a continuance in the union . . . . I have no hesitation in saying, 'Let us separate.'"

After Vice President Burr killed Alexander Hamilton in a duel over personal comments arising out of their political antagonism, he attempted to instigate a private invasion to overthrow Spanish rule in the Southwest and install himself as the king of Mexico. Believing Burr intended to force the secession of the new western states and Louisiana and create an independent nation centered on the Mississippi River, President Jefferson ordered him arrested for treason. In a demonstration of judicial independence, Burr was acquitted by Chief Justice John Marshall.

Most people indentified themselves with their own states, and Union and Confederate regiments in the Civil War were primarily recruited and deployed by states. The question about the right of states to secede from the United States, once admitted, was answered in a practical sense by the Civil War. Constitutionally, the U.S. Supreme Court ruled in 1869 that the words "to form a more perfect Union" in the Constitution conveyed an indissoluble unity.

Manifest Destiny

Along the same philosophical lines as Jacksonian democracy, was the popular belief that the United States had a Manifest Destiny to "extend freedom" to all of the continent. The principle was achieved through a combination of immigration, occupation, purchase and conquest.

Texas won its independence from Mexico in 1836, and its annexation as a state by the United States in 1845 led to the Mexican-American War in 1846. The peace treaty in 1848 resulted in the ceding of territory by Mexico consisting of the present-day states of New Mexico, Arizona, Colorado, Utah, Nevada and California. The lower part of New Mexico and Arizona was purchased from Mexico in 1853.

A treaty with England in 1846 extinguished British claims to the Oregon territory, including the states of Oregon, Washington, Idaho, and parts of Montana and Wyoming.

Based upon its exploration and fur trading operations, Russia claimed Alaska; however, concerns about a possible war with

England motivated Russia to sell Alaska to the United States in 1867. The price paid for the territory was $7.2 million, or about two-and-a-half cents an acre—an even better deal than the Louisiana Purchase.

The independent Kingdom of Hawaii was overthrown by American businessmen and planters, who established a republic in 1894. It became a territory of the United States in 1898.

The political question debated in most of these acquisitions, was whether slavery would be allowed in the new territories and states. That unresolved issue ultimately required the deaths of 750,000 northern and southern soldiers to settle.

The Power of Political Parties

The Democratic and Whig political parties became national powers, with professional party managers directing operations, soliciting and disbursing funds, and organizing voter turnouts. Presidential elections became masterful spectacles of torchlight parades, fireworks and speeches—all fueled by generous supplies of liquor. More than 80 percent of eligible white males turned out to vote in the election of 1840.

Many came to consider the two-party system as a "Second Constitution," in which party leaders seeking votes were forced to respond to the needs of the People. Ideally, each party recognized the legitimacy of the other. As administrative decision-making became more centralized in Washington, DC, the power of petition and party began to give way to that of the paid lobby.

The Whigs believed the federal government should actively take steps—such as building canals and roads and encouraging the construction of railroads and telegraphs—to increase individual and business opportunities. A country lawyer in Illinois,

Abraham Lincoln, took up the Whig banner in saying the "legitimate object of government, is to do for a community of people, whatever they need to have done, but cannot do, at all, or cannot, so well do, for themselves—in their separate, and individual capacities." Unsurprisingly, he began to get more legal business representing railroad corporations.

Almost 3,000 miles of railroads had been laid down in the United States by the 1840s, and by 1860, more than 30,000 miles were in operation. These lines not only revolutionized the transportation of people, goods and commodities, but they connected villages and sectors of the country—allowing a greater freedom of individual movement. The more rapid diffusion of knowledge and information encouraged the development of public education.

Public Education

Writing on the relationship between authority and liberty, the English philosopher John Stuart Mill emphasized the importance of individuality in the pursuit of happiness. Fearing a combination of rich men, Mill believed worker's cooperatives would allow individual working men and women to gain economic control of their lives. Mill thought education was the foundation of individual freedom, and he believed in the political contribution of exceptional, well-educated individuals. He said, "What is right in politics, is not the will of the people, but the good of the people."

In proposing a national university, George Washington said, "it is essential that public opinion should be enlightened." Thomas Jefferson went further:

I know of no safe depository of the ultimate powers of the society, but the people themselves: and if we think them not enlightened enough to exercise their control with a wholesome discretion, the remedy is, not to take it from them, but to inform their discretion by education. This is the true corrective of abuses of constitutional power.

Initially, following the Revolution, primary education was offered by churches; however, Massachusetts was the first state to establish nonsectarian schools to teach the basics to all children. Laws mandating compulsory public education were passed in many states, and most came to provide free elementary education—at least in the cities.

Horace Mann, who established the first common schools, taught that education was "the great equalizer of the conditions of men" and it "prevents [them from] being poor." Basic literacy became widespread, and at least half of all households subscribed to newspapers by the 1820s.

Failing to benefit from any of these educational efforts were the three million African-American slaves held in human bondage in the United States. In most southern states, it was against the law to educate slaves. With owners holding the power of life and death, seeking enlightenment could be capital offense for slaves, and there was no appeal from an owner's judgment.

Abraham Lincoln, the New Republican Party, and the End of Slavery

Although it had been English investors and ship owners, primarily, who had gotten rich from the slave trade between Africa and the Americas, England banned the trade in 1807 and abolished slavery throughout the British Empire in 1833. The English debate was driven by the Enlightenment belief that all humans possessed natural rights and by the conviction of certain religious groups, especially the Quakers, that slavery was a moral sin.

In the United States, the abolition movement and the female suffrage movement were united in many northern cities, with the establishment of female antislavery societies and the circulation of petitions. There was a fear in the North that Jacksonian democracy represented a takeover of the nation by Southern slave interests.

By 1837, there were more than 1,000 abolitionist societies taking advantage of the modern press and rail transportation to quickly disseminate their messages. Jackson—who owned more than 150 slaves—attempted to obtain a censorship law prohibiting abolitionist materials from the mail, and his postmasters were encouraged to exclude "incendiary" materials.

John Quincy Adams, who served Massachusetts in the House of Representatives after his presidency, spoke often on the right of petition, particularly by women—who had no other voice in government. The political experience gained by women participating in the abolitionist movement would serve them well in their future campaign to obtain suffrage.

The current Republican Party was formed in 1854 to oppose the expansion of slavery in the new western states. Its formation represented a failure of the existing two-party system to deal with the issue of slavery in a manner that satisfied the members of both parties. The Republicans quickly rose to political prominence in the Northeast and upper Midwest, as the Whig Party disintegrated.

Although the two parties would undergo philosophical and regional changes in the future, the new Republican and Democratic Parties have the same lineage as today's parties. Continuing through the Civil War and Reconstruction, the era is referred to as the "Third Party System."

The Growth of Freedom

In 1858, Abraham Lincoln abandoned the Whig Party and became the Republican candidate for the U.S. Senate seat from Illinois held by the Northern Democrat Stephen Douglas. The two engaged in a series of public debates, which were widely reported in the newspapers. Although Lincoln lost the election in the Illinois legislature, he became recognized as a national political figure.

Two years later, in the presidential election of 1860—with the Democratic Party split between northern and southern candidates—Lincoln won a majority of the Electoral College and was elected president of a seriously divided country. Commencing with South Carolina, which had earlier tried to nullify the federal protective tariff, the southern states—believing they retained the right under the Constitution—began to secede from the United States they had fought to establish.

Lincoln was determined to preserve the union, and as their Commander-in-Chief, he led the great northern armies to ultimate victory. It was the first war to be fought with modern weaponry, and it was bloody beyond belief. Not only did more than 750,000 Union and Confederate soldiers die as a consequence of the war, but more than 50,000 civilians perished as well. Soldiers on both sides referred to the killing as "work," and the labor of several millions of working soldiers was prodigious. The horror of the war reached into every household, leaving a "republic of suffering," which has yet to be reconciled.

Lincoln's entire first term was consumed fighting the war, as his mission slowly expanded from preserving the union, to ending slavery. With his Emancipation Proclamation in 1863, Lincoln declared the freedom of all slaves in the rebellious states. It did not emancipate the one million slaves in other states, but Lincoln ordered the enrollment of former slaves into 166 Union regiments of black troops.

In the presidential election of 1864, Lincoln easily won re-election in the Electoral College, especially as there were no votes from the southern states.

The surrender of the Army of Virginia by General Robert E. Lee at Appomattox to General Ulysses S. Grant on April 9, 1865 ended major combat operations. Lincoln began to make plans for the recovery of the nation, and in a speech on April 11, he concluded by saying, "I am considering, and shall not fail to act, when satisfied that action will be proper." Speaking afterwards, he said it was "his firm resolution to stand for clemency against all opposition."

Lincoln did not want to punish the South, or change its social structure, but he did want the Thirteenth Amendment to the Constitution to be ratified. The Amendment—which effectively extended the Emancipation Proclamation to free all slaves in the United States—had just passed the House of Representatives and was to be submitted to the states, including those in the South. It stated:

Neither slavery nor involuntary servitude, except as a punishment for crime whereof the party shall have been duly convicted, shall exist within the United States, or any place subject to their jurisdiction.

The murder of Abraham Lincoln on April 14 changed everything. Waving the "bloody shirt," Radical Republicans obtained a majority in Congress in 1866 and imposed harsh terms on the South. Relying on the votes of newly enfranchised freedmen and the disenfranchisement of rebels, Republicans seized political power throughout the South—where they were reinforced by the Union Army.

Following his election in 1868, President Grant supported the Radical Reconstruction of the South. Defeat in the Civil War was a harsh blow to Southern pride; however, the brutal treatment of the South unnecessarily created bitterness and hatred that would endure for another century, at least.

Due Process and Equal Protection of the Law

There was concern about the number and allocation of representatives, which would result in Congress once the full number of former slaves was counted, rather than the three-fifths authorized in the Constitution. Moreover, in response to southern legislation and other acts restricting the movement and voting rights of former slaves, Congress proposed another constitutional amendment to guarantee due process and equal protection of the law in the South.

As a sanction, the proposed amendment reduced the number of a state's representatives and electors—should the right of former slaves vote be interfered with—and it denied the right of former rebels to serve in Congress or the presidency.

The most significant provision was Section One:

All persons born or naturalized in the United States, and subject to the jurisdiction thereof, are citizens of the United States and of the State wherein they reside. No State shall make or enforce any law which shall abridge the privileges or immunities of citizens of the United States; nor shall any State deprive any person of life, liberty, or property, without due process of law; nor deny to any person within its jurisdiction the equal protection of the laws.

Initially, the southern states refused to ratify the Amendment; however, Congress acted to deny representation to the rebel states, until they ratified the Fourteenth Amendment. It was declared ratified in 1868.

To ensure the vote of freedmen in the South, which was important to the electoral success of the Republican Party, the Fifteenth Amendment was passed and ratified two years later. It held that:

> The right of citizens of the United States to vote shall not be denied or abridged by the United States or by any State on account of race, color, or previous condition of servitude.

All three of these amendments were designed to protect natural persons—who had been previously held in slavery or involuntary servitude—not corporations. As the Civil War was ending, Lincoln became frightened by the great power gained by corporations during the war. His fears were not misplaced, as the due process and equal protection clause of the Fourteenth Amendment would soon be denied to the "natural persons" it was designed to protect, and it was hijacked by "corporate persons," for whom it was never intended.

The new constitutional guarantee of a freedman's right to vote, did not improve the general voting rights of all citizens. The Constitution continued to allow the right to vote to be controlled by the states. Under the Fifteenth Amendment, the states were not allowed to discriminate on the basis of race, color or previous condition of servitude; however, they could impose other restrictions on voting, which had the same effect.

Protection of African-American voting in the South depended upon its occupation by the U.S. Army, and Reconstruction collapsed when the Army was evacuated in 1877. The withdrawal was pursuant to a congressional compromise allowing the election of the Republican candidate, Rutherford B. Hayes, who had lost the popular vote and failed to achieve a majority of the Electoral College. His selection in the House of Representatives depended upon the votes of southern Democrats, who exerted their newly restored power.

A contemporary cartoon depicted the Democratic donkey clothed in a lion's skin frightening all of the other animals, including an elephant labeled as the Republican Party. The cartoon established the elephant as the Republican mascot.

Democrats quickly regained political dominance in the South and passed "Jim Crow" laws effectively depriving African Americans of their constitutional rights. These laws included discriminatory literacy tests, the imposition of poll taxes and a "whites only" primary system. Some of these laws were later reversed; however, African Americans remained effectively disenfranchised in the South for almost a century.

In *Plessy v. Ferguson*, the U.S. Supreme Court upheld the constitutionality of state segregation laws. In the 1896 case, the Court ruled "separate but equal" public facilities did not violate the due process and equal protection provisions of the Fourteenth Amendment. Sixty years later, Justice Hugo Black remarked that less than one half of one percent of all due process litigation involved protection of the "Negro race" and that "more than fifty percent asked its benefits be extended to corporations."

The Growth of Corporate Power

In 1816, the state of New Hampshire attempted to convert Dartmouth College from a private to a public institution. The trustees retained Daniel Webster to represent them, and the matter was ultimately decided in the U.S. Supreme Court. Chief Justice John Marshall ruled that the original charter granted by the King of England to the Board of Trustees was a contract between private parties and that New Hampshire could not interfere with the contract. The decision was based on the sanctity of a contract—not whether a Board of Trustees, as a nonperson corporate entity, was a proper subject for constitutional protection.

In a California legal case, in which a county attempted to collect taxes from a railroad company, the corporation alleged a deprivation of due process and equal protection under the Fourteenth Amendment. The matter was appealed to the U.S. Supreme Court in 1886.

The case was decided on the basis of whether the county could properly tax the fences that lined the railroad, and the constitutional due process issue was not a part of the written opinion. The court clerk, however, in summarizing the case in a headnote erroneously wrote these fateful words:

> One of the points made and discussed at length in the brief of counsel for defendants in error was that "corporations are persons within the meaning of the Fourteenth Amendment to the Constitution of the United States." Before argument, Mr. Chief Justice Waite said: The court does not wish to hear argument on the question whether the provision in the Fourteenth Amendment to the Constitution, which forbids a State to deny to any person within its jurisdiction the equal

protection of the laws, applies to these corporations. We are all of the opinion that it does.

From these humble beginnings and without a basis in the Constitution or the Court's decision, the doctrine became established that corporations were persons within the meaning of the Fourteenth Amendment of the Constitution. Thus, an amendment originally intended to protect the least powerful of natural persons was shamefully corrupted to shield the most powerful corporate persons—at a time when the constitutional rights of the people for whom the amendment was written were no longer being protected.

In an attempt to avoid state laws limiting the size of corporations, John D. Rockefeller created a trust company in 1882 to control corporations he had organized in various states. The Standard Oil Trust came to dominate 95 percent of all refined oil shipments.

When Ohio brought an antitrust action against Standard Oil, Rockefeller reincorporated in New Jersey, which had less restrictive laws. New Jersey allowed holding companies, in which corporations could buy and sell the stock of other companies and exchange their own stock as payment. As a part of its permissive laws regulating corporations, New Jersey rescinded its 55-year limit on the life of corporations, permitting them to do business in any state or country in perpetuity. It also allowed the issuance of nonvoting stock, which enabled the major shareholders of corporations to maintain close control. After first expressing outrage, other states quickly followed New Jersey's lead.

Woodrow Wilson attempted to regain some control over corporations when he was governor of New Jersey; however, the corporations simply moved next door to Delaware. Today, more than half of the largest corporations in the Fortune 500 are incorporated in Delaware. The state's total registration of 945,326 corporations, is more than its population of people.

States that issue corporate charters have the power to revoke them if they become a danger to the public; however, the states have shown little interest in rescinding corporate charters, except for a failure to pay fees or taxes.

Extending the Suffrage

Under the Constitution, members of the House of Representatives were the only federal offices directly elected by the people. All other offices were indirectly elected, including the two U.S. senators from each state, who were elected by their state legislatures.

Constitutional amendments calling for direct elections of senators were introduced in 1828, 1829 and 1855, but it was not until the end of the Nineteenth Century that the matter was seriously considered. After 31 state legislatures voted to reform the process, and a Second Constitutional Convention was threatened, Congress was finally forced to act. A constitutional amendment was passed in 1912, and the Seventeenth Amendment was ratified the following year, allowing most men, and a few women, to directly vote for their senators.

It would take a while longer for most American women to be allowed to vote for their electoral choices.

Writing to her husband in 1776, as John Adams was working on the Declaration of Independence, Abigail Adams said she was pleased with the idea of independence, but asked:

—and by the way in the new code of laws which I suppose it will be necessary for you to make, I desire you would remember the ladies, and be more favorable to them than your ancestors. Do not put such unlimited power into the hands of husbands.

Adams, who probably had a better and more loving relationship with his wife than any of the other founding fathers, responded that he "cannot but laugh," and went on to say:

We have been told that our struggle has loosened the bands of government everywhere; that children and apprentices were disobedient; that schools and colleges were grown turbulent; that Indians slighted their guardians and Negroes grew insolent to their masters. But your letter was the first intimation that another tribe more numerous and powerful than all the rest were grown discontented. This is rather too coarse a compliment but you are so saucy, I won't blot it out.

Depend on it, we know better than to repeal our masculine systems. Although they are in full force, you know they are little more than theory. We dare not exert our power in its full latitude. We are obliged to go fair and softly, and in practice you know we are the subjects. We have only the name of masters, and rather than give up this, which would completely subject us to the despotism of the petticoat, I hope General Washington and all our brave heroes would fight.

Only New Jersey allowed women to vote following the Revolution; however, in 1807 that right was withdrawn. It would take the abolitionist movement to sufficiently involve women in political matters and for them to raise the issue of their own right to vote.

Commencing in 1848 with the Seneca Falls Convention, women activists began to agitate for their right to vote. Following the Civil War and ratification of the Fourteenth and Fifteenth Amendments, women were able to point to the failure of the Constitution to protect the voting rights of half of the people in the United States.

Since the individual states had the power to grant women suffrage, the movement first targeted the states. Wyoming (1869) and Utah (1870) were the first to allow women to vote; however, Utah women were disenfranchised by the anti-Mormon laws of 1887. By the end of the century, Idaho and Colorado had also extended the franchise to women.

Susan B. Anthony, one of the leading women activists, claimed protection of the Fourteenth Amendment saying, "All persons are citizens—and no state shall deny or abridge the citizen rights." When she went to the polls and cast a protest vote in 1872, Anthony was arrested and brought to trial. The judge disallowed her testimony because she was a female and convicted her of illegally voting.

With the presidential election of Woodrow Wilson, women suffragists took their protests to the steps of the White House. Wilson attempted to ignore the women, and many of them were arrested, jailed and abused. As a war measure, he reluctantly endorsed women suffrage in 1918.

First introduced in 1878, the enabling congressional legislation was not enacted until 1919, when the proposed amendment was sent to the states for ratification. The Nineteenth Amendment was ratified the following year. Profound in its simplicity, it says: "The right of citizens of the United States to vote shall not be denied or abridged by the United States or by any State on account of sex." The Amendment implies that "citizens" have the right to vote. In reality, it only provided women the same voting rights as men, which could be denied or abridged for other reasons by the states.

The Progressive Era

In the later part of the Nineteenth Century, progressive Republicans more often supported reform and government-funded programs, while conservative Democrats believed in individual initiative, rather than government solutions. The North was generally Republican, while the "solid South" voted Democratic. With time, these philosophical and political positions would become reversed.

As is still the case, membership in the political parties during the later part of the Nineteenth Century consisted of one's own self identification with one party or the other, instead of paying dues. People fervently supported their party, turning out for barbeques and parades, playing in political bands or singing in glee clubs, and helping to turn out the vote. Most newspapers contained political news, and voter participation was at an all-time high.

Parties printed paper ballots, which were handed out to voters by party activists at the entrance to the polls, along with cash or chits for drinks at a local saloon. The ballots contained only the names of the parties' nominees, and poll watchers could follow voters inside and ensure party ballots were dropped in collection boxes. If a voter had the courage to do so, he could scratch out the name of a nominee and write in his own choice. Voting was anything but secret.

In rural areas, voting was a holiday affair, with farmers and their families coming together in small towns for one of the few days of the year when they could all get together.

Candidates for all offices were nominated through a caucus system that extended from villages all the way through the state level to the national presidential conventions. It was in these "smoke-filled back rooms" where decisions about party candidates were made.

With increased public literacy, parties began to print and distribute pamphlets devoted to specific issues or political platforms. These publications were often directed toward undecided or independent voters. Parties could pretty much count on their faithful supporters, but elections were often decided by "floaters." Politics began to move from entertaining voters to educating them, and parties became more receptive to reform movements.

The period of political reform commencing in the 1890s is known as the Progressive Era and is referred to as the "Fourth Party System."

Beginning around the turn of the century, the states began to legislate in favor of replacing party caucuses with the popular nomination of candidates in primary elections. By the first world war, the majority of states had direct primaries, and most included all state offices on the primary ballots. Following the Seventeenth Amendment—which allowed the direct election of senators by popular vote—more and more states began to include the nomination of representatives, senators, and presidential candidates in the primary process.

Strongly supported by organized labor, states also began to adopt the "Australian ballot." Printed by local governments—instead of political parties—standard, uniform ballots were distributed by election officials at the polls. Party activists were not allowed inside polling places, and ballots could be marked in secret.

The cost of conducting elections was shifted from political parties to local and state governments; however, the process strengthened the two major parties by making it more difficult for small parties to qualify for the ballot.

A further reform was the inclusion of state constitutional amendments, referenda, initiatives and other propositions on the ballots for decisions by the voters. All of these measures increased the complexity of the ballots, and parties began to organize classes to educate voters on how to properly mark their ballots. The major newspapers followed suit and printed sample ballots on the news pages, along with instructions. Voters could clip the articles and take them to the polls. Most newspapers continued to exhibit a political bias, which they expressed in the form of editorial endorsements for candidates and propositions.

Led by the League of Women Voters, reform efforts encouraged state and local governments to distribute independent information bulletins containing the arguments for and against the various initiatives and propositions that voters were expected to decide.

Both major political parties continued to reward the party faithful with government jobs in payment for their support in elections. For many voters and activists, patronage was more important than political issues. Political appointees from both parties were expected to contribute a portion of their salaries to maintain their parties. With civil service reform, a shift was made towards the solicitation of larger contributions from a more select and wealthy group of political supporters.

As the Progressive Era and its political reforms extended into the Twentieth Century, a fundamental shift had taken place in politics. Although participatory democracy through voting had been expanded, the personal involvement of voters had been reduced. The operation of political parties was assumed by professional managers, and political candidacy became a career path. With less involvement in elections, the time and attention of most voters shifted from the passion of politics to the more mundane problems of work and family.

The United States had become a major player on the world stage. The federal government, rather than state and local governments, was expected to solve more of the People's problems. Political parties became more focused on national, rather than state and local issues. Politics became an occasional trip to the polls by most voters to make a choice between the policies and candidates proposed by the two parties.

Voters had gained the independence to "split the ticket" and chose the best person for the job, irrespective of party. The reality was that government policy was increasingly made by the Republican and Democratic parties, rather than the candidates they put forth. People came to vote for the candidates of the party that best represented a voter's political philosophy, irrespective of the individual qualifications of the candidates.

Both parties became more dependent on the same powerful corporate interests for the money required to operate. Their policies reflected the demands of those special interests, rather than the protection of the People—who suffered from the actions of those interests.

Much like today, the nation was confronted with massive social and political issues during the "Roaring Twenties," including a growing disparity of income and wealth; an unregulated banking and stock market system; and low voter turnouts.

Political issues were becoming complicated beyond the ability of many voters to comprehend, and the policy platforms of the parties increasingly offered fewer alternatives. Most farmers, laborers, and small business owners were working far too hard in their daily struggle to feed, clothe and shelter their families to think about politics. The career politicians were too busy collecting legalized bribes to help people with their most basic needs.

Paid professional lobbyists, often representing narrow corporate interests, gained enormous power and prestige in the federal government through their ability to funnel money to politicians. Lobbyists were referred to as the "third house of Congress," and voters became less important than those who hired the lobbyists. Reform legislation requiring the registration of lobbyists and a statement of their purposes failed to obtain sufficient support for passage.

America learned the value of political propaganda during World War I to get people, accustomed to isolationism, to fight in an overseas war that seemed to have little to do with their daily lives. Commercial propaganda—in the form of publicity and advertising agencies—was adopted by political parties to secure voter support.

Public relations specialists and their press releases began to play a greater role in the molding of public opinion, both for consumer products and for political issues. The image of candidates became more important than what they really believed or had to say.

Just as the advertising costs of companies selling soap and automobiles consumed a large portion of their sales budgets, paying for the manipulation of voter opinions and favorable legislation brought ever-increasing "contributions" from corporate "supporters." As early as 1905, Theodore Roosevelt proposed a ban on all corporate contributions to political campaigns:

I again recommend a law prohibiting all corporations from contributing to the campaign expenses of any party . . . . Let individuals contribute as they desire, but let us prohibit in effective fashion all corporations from making contributions for any political purposes, directly or indirectly.

State and federal laws were enacted imposing spending limits and ordering the disclosure of contributions over a certain amount. Enforcement was lacking in most cases, and corporate bribery through campaign financing continued unabated.

As society became more complicated and industrialization posed greater dangers to public health, national solutions were sought. Federal regulatory and enforcement agencies—and the laws and regulations they enforced—began to directly impinge upon the lives of ordinary people.

With the shift to federal intervention, the role of the president came to personify the government. The president was the person who said he had the answers, and he was the person hired to do the job.

The focus of power within the federal government shifted from the Legislative to the Executive Branch, and it became expected that the president would lead the nation, formulate its policies, and obtain legislation and regulations to effectuate his policies. Like a successful businessman, the president was expected to surround himself with smart people and to translate and manage their opinions and ideas into effective plans of action.

Just as civil service reform sought to employ and promote non-politically-appointed public employees based upon examinations and merit, universities began to educate students to specialize in social and political science. These people came to understand how the research and formulation of policy was an integral part of professional careers working in government for the public benefit.

With the crash of the stock market in 1929, followed by the Great Depression and the establishment of communism in Russia and fascism in Germany, Italy, and Japan, the people of the United States were ready for someone to lead them through the social and political chaos toward a better life.

Franklin D. Roosevelt and the New Deal

One-third of the nation was without income during the presidential election of 1932, in which Franklin D. Roosevelt, a masterful politician, offered Americans a New Deal with their government. The People bought the contract, and Roosevelt reassured them that they had "nothing to fear but fear itself." He proposed a government that accepted responsibility for the lives of its people.

Faced with a complete disintegration of American society and confronted with the reality of violent revolution, Roosevelt enlisted hundreds of volunteer "dollar-a-year" executives to help manage and mobilize government resources, and he brought thousands of social scientists and economists into his administration.

Roosevelt motivated a Democratic majority in Congress to accomplish the "Three Rs." He sought to provide *relief* for those who were poor and unemployed, help the economy *recover* to previous levels of productivity, and *reform* the financial system to prevent further crashes.

The Democratic Party became the dominant political party in America, bringing together the white voters of the "Solid South," organized labor, Northern blacks (who had historically voted Republican), and big-city political machines.

The Republican Party split between traditional conservatives—who opposed Roosevelt's programs—and its moderate members, who understood that drastic steps had to be taken to save the nation and its people.

A second wave of New Deal programs in 1935-1936 brought increased support for labor unions and fair labor standards, and improved relief programs for farmers and unemployed workers. The Social Security Act was enacted, providing for old age and disability security. Passage of these programs in Congress was made possible by the prevalence of liberal and moderate New Deal Democrats, Republicans, and independents in Congress, sufficient to overcome the opposition of conservatives in both parties.

With the loss of the super majority in 1938 and 1940, there were some program reversals. The economy finally began to recover as mobilization for the war effort kicked in, and there was full employment of the nation's human resources.

Rather than an administration run by the Democratic Party, the New Deal achieved a more professional and nonpartisan government that worked for the People. Legislation in 1940 ensured that 95 percent of federal employees worked under the merit-based civil service system, and the Hatch Acts of 1939 and 1940 restricted most federal employees from engaging in political activities.

Roosevelt was a master communicator, speaking directly to the people through his weekly fireside chats on the radio, and indirectly through intimate press conferences in his office with selected journalists. Although he had little use of his legs as a result of polio, his disabilities were never discussed in public, and the image of his great strength reassured the People.

On January 6, 1941, with war looming on the horizon, President Roosevelt informed Congress and the People about the State of the Union. Instead of asking for a declaration of war on the fascist nations, he called upon the United States to become an "Arsenal of Democracy" to help the Allies defend themselves against fascism. He said:

> In the future days, which we seek to make secure, we look forward to a world founded upon four essential human freedoms.

> The first is freedom of speech and expression—everywhere in the world.

> The second is freedom of every person to worship God in his own way—everywhere in the world.

> The third is freedom from want—which, translated into world terms, means economic understandings which will secure to every nation a healthy peacetime life for its inhabitants—everywhere in the world.

> The fourth is freedom from fear—which, translated into world terms, means a worldwide reduction in armaments to such a point and in such a thorough fashion that no nation

will be in a position to commit an act of physical aggression against any neighbor—anywhere in the world.

The Four Freedoms of speech and expression, of worship, from want, and from fear, became the unifying spirit of the American People, as they were forcibly drawn into the war.

Following the Japanese attack on Pearl Harbor on December 7, 1941, the United States organized itself for fighting in Europe and the Pacific Ocean. The national defense budget increased from $1.5 billion in 1940 to $81.5 billion in 1945. Spurred by this investment, the Gross National Product doubled from $99.7 billion in 1940 to $212 billion in 1945.

Sixteen million—one in every eight—Americans, including 350,000 women, served in the U.S. military. The labor force increased to a peak of 55 million in 1943, as Americans manufactured 1,600 warships, almost 6,000 merchant vessels, 100,000 tanks and armored vehicles, 635,000 jeeps and 15,000,000 guns. By the end of the war, America was building 100,000 airplanes a year.

The war was paid for by loans from the People in the form of war bonds and through tax revenues, including an income tax based on payroll withholding.

Women and minorities joined the labor force in large numbers and secured an increase in social status. For the United States, the war ended with its industrial capacity intact, and its people had savings to spend and unfulfilled consumer desires to satisfy. Military men were demobilized and reentered the job market. The question was whether the nation could organize for peace, as well as it had for war?

Freedom and the American Dream

Roosevelt was reelected to an unprecedented fourth term. The presence of progressive and moderate elements in both major parties allowed the government to be professionally organized to attend to the needs of the vast majority of the American people.

The political alignment of special interest groups and philosophical factions within the parties continued after the war through several presidential administrations by both parties. It contributed to one of the greatest periods of freedom and peacetime prosperity ever experienced by any nation or people. The period is generally known as the "Fifth Party System."

President Roosevelt did not live to see the end of the war; however, within weeks of Japan's surrender, President Harry Truman reaffirmed the nation's commitment to the Four Freedoms. He sought to raise the minimum wage, extend unemployment compensation, and launch major public works projects. He sent a message to Congress urging the creation of a national health insurance fund for Americans over the age of 65; however, Congress failed to act.

For almost eight years, Truman presided over a postwar economic boom in which many, if not most, American families came to enjoy a comfortable life style primarily paid for by a husband's single income. A vigorous labor movement, supported by government oversight and regulation, improved the salaries and benefits of all working people. Organized labor obtained better and safer working conditions, medical and retirement benefits, a standard five-day, 40-hour work week, overtime and holiday pay, worker's compensation and fair employment standards.

The GI Bill of Rights enabled thousands of veterans to obtain professional educations and low-cost home mortgages.

Most Americans felt secure in their lives and confident of the future. They were living the American Dream.

When President Truman left office in 1952, the only income he had was his Army pension of $112 a month, and he was not provided any government support, including secret service protection. When offered large salaries to join several corporations, he refused saying, "You don't want me. You want the office of the president, and that doesn't belong to me. It belongs to the American people and it's not for sale." Returning home to Independence, Missouri, Truman drove his own car and mowed his own front lawn. The imperial presidency had yet to arrive in America.

Representing the moderate wing of the Republican Party, President Dwight Eisenhower continued the Fifth Party System through the massive public works construction of the Interstate Highway System and the Saint Lawrence Seaway. The projects were paid for by a gasoline tax and the issuance of bonds. His main purpose was "to build up a strong progressive Republican Party in this Country. If the right wing wants a fight, they are going to get it."

Eisenhower also said:

Should any political party attempt to abolish social security, unemployment insurance, and eliminate labor laws and farm programs, you would not hear of that party again in our political history. There is a tiny splinter group, of course, that believes that you can do these things. Among them are a few Texas oil millionaires, and an occasional politician or businessman from other areas. Their number is negligible and they are stupid.

President Eisenhower continued the New Deal agencies and consolidated them in a new Department of Health, Education and Welfare. Social Security benefits were increased and coverage was expanded to include millions of beneficiaries. Federal funding for public education was increased; federal troops were deployed to enforce court orders desegregating schools in the South; and the military was completely desegregated. These programs were underwritten by high corporate taxes—which accounted for one quarter of federal revenues.

Enjoying their sweet dreams, Americans purchased new homes in the suburbs, mothers remained at home raising healthy and well-adjusted children, who attended newly constructed neighborhood schools and walked home to play on safe streets. Americans bought the latest gadgets, especially televisions, which became widely available. The era was epitomized by *The Life of Riley*, a radio and television sitcom, that featured an ordinary assembly line worker in an Southern California aircraft plant living the good life and relaxing in his backyard hammock.

Life was also becoming easier down on the farms, with electricity, telephones, and other utilities being delivered by the Tennessee Valley Authority, the Rural Electrification Administration, and the Rural Utilities Service. The Department of Agriculture assisted small farmers to become more productive and successful, and they became better connected by the free delivery of mail to most homesteads.

The median income of all households doubled between 1947 and 1973. This provided greater privacy for families, whose parents had the social security to live alone to older ages, and whose young people had better opportunities to leave home and to make it on their own. Fringe benefits for workers were expanded, including an increase in private pensions—from 3.8

million in 1940 to 15.2 million in 1956—and workers with medical insurance increased from 6 million to 91 million in the same period.

Increased incomes allowed mothers to remain at home with their children in most middle-class families—if they chose to do so. Nonetheless, the freedom gained by women to work outside the home during World War II, and the status it provided, was not forgotten. The percentage of women attending college increased, as did their participation in the workforce. Women primarily found outside employment as secretaries, nurses or teachers, but they were also moving into medicine, law, and engineering. Even so, women continued to carry the primary burden of childrearing and housekeeping, and their salaries never equaled that of men in the same or similar positions.

Dwight Eisenhower considered himself to be a "modern Republican," who accepted the New Deal. He believed there was a great danger in economic inequality and that government should "prevent or correct abuses springing from the unregulated practice of a private economy."

President Eisenhower signed the first voting rights legislation since Reconstruction in 1957, which prohibited intimidating, coercing, or otherwise interfering with the rights of persons to vote for the President and members of Congress. Just before leaving office in 1960, he signed another civil rights act that allowed federal inspection of voting rolls and prohibited the obstruction of voter registration. The purpose of these laws was to reverse the laws and practices in the South that had effectively disenfranchised African Americans.

Following the end of the Korean War, the nation remained at peace during the duration of the Eisenhower administration; however, the military continually pushed the president to ignite the cold war against communism. Eisenhower was pressured to authorize flights of B-47 nuclear bombers over the U.S.S.R. to test its radar defenses and U-2 flights by the CIA to perform high-altitude aerial reconnaissance.

In his final presidential speech, Eisenhower said: "the Congress and the Administration have, on most vital issues, cooperated well, to serve the national good rather than mere partisanship, and so have assured that the business of the Nation should go forward." His remarks included a prophetic warning:

> This conjunction of an immense military establishment and a large arms industry is new in the American experience. The total influence—economic, political, even spiritual—is felt in every city, every State house, every office of the Federal government. We recognize the imperative need for this development. Yet we must not fail to comprehend its grave implications. Our toil, resources and livelihood are all involved; so is the very structure of our society.

> In the councils of government, we must guard against the acquisition of unwarranted influence, whether sought or unsought, by the military-industrial complex. The potential for the disastrous rise of misplaced power exists and will persist.

> We must never let the weight of this combination endanger our liberties or democratic processes. We should take nothing for granted. Only an alert and knowledgeable citizenry can compel the proper meshing of the huge industrial and military machinery of defense with our peaceful methods and goals, so that security and liberty may prosper together.

The defeat of Vice President Richard Nixon by Senator John Kennedy in 1960 returned the presidency to the Democratic Party, and the Fifth Party System remained intact. In his first State of the Union address in 1961, President Kennedy stated:

> The denial of constitutional rights to some of our fellow Americans on account of race—at the ballot box and elsewhere—disturbs the national conscience, and subjects us to the charge of world opinion that our democracy is not equal to the high promise of our heritage.

In August 1963, more than 100,000 demonstrators joined a March on Washington for Jobs and Freedom. The protest was peaceful, and its leaders met with Kennedy in the White House. He had earlier delivered a civil rights speech calling for legislation to end segregation in schools and public facilities, and increased protection of voting rights. President Kennedy was assassinated in November 1963 before the legislation could be enacted.

Involvement of the CIA and military in the assassination continues to be one of the major conspiracy theories regarding the murder. President Kennedy was faulted by them for refusing to authorize air attacks of Cuba in support of the CIA-trained counter-revolutionary army during the Bay of Pigs invasion. In addition, Kennedy quashed a treasonous plan by the Pentagon to use false-flag terrorist attacks to justify a direct military invasion of Cuba. Operation Northwoods had recommended the sinking of "a boatload of Cubans enroute to Florida (real or simulated). We could foster attempts on lives of Cuban refugees in the United States even to the extent of wounding . . . [by] exploding a few plastic bombs."

Vice President Lyndon Johnson succeeded to the presidency. He had generally served a conservative agenda during his 30 years in Congress as a Southern Democrat from Texas, including blocking President Truman's attempt to obtain civil rights legislation. Johnson was a masterful politician, who had been the powerful leader of his party in the Senate. Because of his personal and political relationships, Johnson had great leverage in Congress and was able to overcome Southern opposition in achieving significant civil rights legislation during his time in office.

President Johnson was able to move Kennedy's civil rights proposal through Congress by the exercise of clever parliamentary tactics and the loyalty of his old friends in the Congress. As he signed the Civil Rights Act of 1964—shrewd politician that he was—Johnson said, "We [the Democrats] have lost the South for a generation."

Following his landslide reelection in 1964, Johnson spoke in favor of an additional Voting Rights Act:

Rarely are we met with the challenge . . . to the values and the purposes and the meaning of our beloved nation. The issue of equal rights for American Negroes is such an issue. And should we defeat every enemy, should we double our wealth and conquer the stars, and still be unequal to this issue, then we will have failed as a people and as a nation.

With passage of the Voting Rights Act of 1965, millions of African Americans in the South were able to vote for the first time, and the number of blacks elected to state and federal offices began to substantially increase. Johnson appointed the first African American to a cabinet position as head of the new Department of Housing and Urban Development.

In his mission to create a Great Society, Johnson obtained a billion dollars in funding for education and launched a War on Poverty by creating the Head Start and food stamp programs. Johnson resurrected Truman's health care proposal for the elderly and pushed it through Congress. Johnson traveled to Independence, Missouri on July 30, 1965 and signed the bill in the Truman Presidential Library. He handed Harry and Bess Truman the first two Medicare cards.

During his last year in office, Johnson signed the Civil Rights Act of 1968, which ensured equal housing opportunities, and he obtained passage of the Fair Housing Act.

The Vietnam War raged throughout the Johnson Administration. Even though he pursued both "guns and butter" programs, discontent and anti-war protests by students contributed to Johnson's decision to not run for re-election. Moreover, the New Deal coalition of the Democratic Party was falling apart—with the labor, anti-war, southerner, and minority factions dividing over continuation of the war and other issues.

The Democrats failed to unite following the assassination of Senator Robert Kennedy, and Republican Richard Nixon won the election in 1968.

Although the Democratic Party suffered from internal divisions, the Fifth Party System remained in effect throughout the Nixon Administration. The moderate and progressive wing of the Republican Party joined the Democratic majority in Congress to continue New Deal programming. Voters organized in support of bipartisan causes, such as ending the war, civil rights, and cleaning up the environment.

Influenced by environmental and political demonstrations by millions of Americans, legislative acts and agencies enacted or created during the Nixon administration included: the Clean Air Act, Clean Water Act, Safe Drinking Water Act, Endangered Species Act, National Environmental Policy Act, the Environmental Protection Agency, the Occupational Safety and Health Administration, the Consumer Product Safety Commission, the National Highway Traffic Safety Administration, and the Mining Enforcement and Safety Administration.

Responding to the massive drafting of young men during the Vietnam War, a student-led movement to reduce the voting age to 18 swept the country. Supported by President Nixon, Congress passed a constitutional amendment and sent it to the states. It was ratified three months later and became the Twenty-sixth Amendment: "The right of citizens of the United States, who are eighteen years of age or older, to vote shall not be denied or abridged by the United States or by any State on account of age." Once again, however, the Amendment only extended an illusionary constitutional right to vote.

Nixon was re-elected with 60 percent of the popular vote in 1972. Unfortunately, unlawful activities by some of his associates during the election, and his attempted cover-up, led to his disgrace and resignation the following year. Vice president Gerald Ford completed Nixon's second term and was defeated for reelection by Jimmy Carter in 1976.

Although President Carter attempted to confront the "political and economic elite" who "shaped decisions and never had to account for mistakes or to suffer from injustice," his progressive program was opposed by the increasing power of corporate interests. Carter's efforts to enact tax and labor law reform and to create a consumer protection agency were defeated; however pro-business legislation to deregulate the airlines, trucking and railroad industries passed and was signed. The Carter administration was plagued with an energy crisis, inflation, recession, and a diplomatic hostage crisis in Iran that diverted the President's personal attention and reduced his popularity.

President Carter was defeated in the 1980 election by Ronald Reagan. The moderate wing of the Republican Party collapsed, and the party was taken over by conservative corporate elements. The Democratic Party came under the influence of neoliberals with a pro-business agenda. It moved to the right, and the progressive and moderate factions in both parties were marginalized.

The American Dream began to fade away, and the New Deal and the Fifth Party Systems broke down. As we shall see, a corporate-led, class war had been declared to reverse the freedoms slowly gained over a half century through these political systems—and to destroy the Dream they had enabled.

THE DESTRUCTION OF FREEDOM

The essential element of the American Dream is that children have the opportunity to achieve a higher standard of living than their parents and to enjoy greater freedoms and a better life in the future. That dream has been shattered during the past forty years, as the standard of living for blue- and white-collar workers and small business owners has fallen, and social and economic upward mobility has been reversed.

Some still live the good life—primarily the upper-middle class and the wealthy—and there are many more who are mired in poverty. Just because there are millions of people in between the poor and the well off, does not mean these people are still enjoying the bounty of the middle class. Those caught in the center have been trampled down by their own government, which is beholden to a small elite group of wealthy individuals and the corporations and financial institutions they control.

The middle class, to the extent it compares to *The Life of Riley*, has been reduced to economic and political impoverishment. Single wage-earning, median-income workers now earn slightly more than the poverty level. Without two incomes, families can no longer buy a home, maintain health insurance, personally care for their young children, provide a college education for their older children, or build a secure retirement.

Workers cannot even afford to live privately in a small clean apartment, without having roommates to share expenses. This does not mean the American Dream is no longer possible—it is just more of a dream and less of a reality.

The ever-rising cost of housing, health care, child care, fuel, higher education, and other necessities—combined with the loss of union protection for most workers and the shifting burden of taxation to workers and small business owners from corporations and the wealthy—has rudely awakened Americans from their Dream. If Chester A. Riley were to wake up from his nap in the backyard hammock today and look around, we might hear his famous catchphrase of indignation, "What a revoltin' development this is."

The current state of affairs is not the result of happenstance—it is the culmination of a deliberate and well-executed plan for economic, political, and social dominance carried out by the very powerful forces that presidents from Jefferson to Eisenhower warned about.

Before his murder, President Lincoln shared a visionary nightmare about the freedom of the nation he was fighting to preserve:

> It has indeed been a trying hour for the Republic; but I see in the near future a crisis approaching that unnerves me and causes me to tremble for the safety of my country.

> As a result of the war, corporations have been enthroned and an era of corruption in high places will follow, and the money power of the country will endeavor to prolong its reign by working upon the prejudices of the people until all wealth is aggregated in a few hands and the Republic is

destroyed. I feel at this moment more anxiety than ever before, even in the midst of war. God grant that my suspicions may prove groundless.

Unfortunately, this dire threat to human freedom has come to reality, and it was caused by the artificial legal entities created to serve the financial and industrial needs of a modern economy. These corporate robots have gained constitutional protection as persons and have eternal lives. They are programmed with greed and endowed with an absence of conscience. Unfeeling robots have launched class warfare against the real People of the United States, and the weapons they deploy are mistrust, prejudice, fear, and terror. Like a viral infection, insatiable robots have invaded the democratic republic, deprived it of its free will, fed upon its energy, and taken control of its government. Unless they are identified, isolated and inoculated against, the corporate robots will ultimately destroy their host.

The Corporate Conspiracy

Richard Nixon, a conservative Republican, occupied the White House in August 1971; however, Corporate America felt it was under attack. Continuation and expansion of Fifth Party System regulatory programs were interfering with the ability of corporations to pollute the air and water, lie to consumers, produce dangerous products, trample on the rights of their workers, and avoid taxes in their quest for ever-increasing profits and executive salaries. Big Business was represented by the U.S. Chamber of Commerce, which decided to do something about it. The Chairman of the Chamber's Education Committee asked one of America's preeminent corporate lawyers to draft a proposed solution.

The responsive memorandum, titled "Attack on American Free Enterprise," not only resulted in a halt to the imagined attack, it reversed 50 years of progressive legislation and destroyed the American system of free enterprise. The memo was written by Lewis F. Powell, Jr. of Virginia, whose primary clients were in the tobacco industry. He urged the Chamber to play an organizational role "in careful long-range planning and implementation, in consistency of action over an indefinite period of years, in the scale of financing available only through joint effort, and in the political power available only through united action and national organizations."

Powell laid out a multi-faceted program of public education about the essential role of American business, but instructed the business community to learn the "lesson that political power is necessary, that such power must be assiduously [*sic*] cultivated; and that when necessary, it must be used aggressively and with determination—without embarrassment and without . . . reluctance."

Recognizing the power of corporate advertising to "influence consumer decisions," Powell urged American businesses "to apply their great talents vigorously." Underwritten by generous contributions from corporations, he outlined the employment of a highly-paid Chamber staff to include professionals "of the great skill in advertising and working with the media, speakers, lawyers and other specialists."

The memo recognized "the judiciary may be the most important instrument for social, economic and political change." The Chamber was encouraged to assemble "a highly competent staff of lawyers" and seek "lawyers of national standing and reputation" to "appear as counsel amicus in the Supreme Court."

Two months after the Chamber launched his plan of attack, President Nixon appointed Lewis Powell to the U.S. Supreme Court. Justice Powell not only devised the litigation, he got to decide the cases.

Implementation of the Powell Plan was immediate and massive in its deployment of economic and political power. Essentially, the corporate class of America thought the working, middle and small-business classes were benefitting too much from the society, and it declared class warfare. It's mobilization and deployment of resources can only be compared to the strategic planning and organization involved in a military offensive.

The Chamber of Commerce created a campaign for capitalism having a mission to "advance human progress through an economic, political and social system based on individual freedom, incentive, initiative, opportunity, and responsibility." The chamber organized thousands of Congressional Action Committees throughout the U.S., which were charged with lobbying their local representatives. It distributed education kits titled "Economics for Young Americans" to its members and encouraged them to place the kits in local schools and to speak to students about the value of capitalism.

The National Association of Manufacturers moved its headquarters from New York City to Washington, DC, in recognizing: "The interrelationship of business with business is no longer so important as the interrelationship of business with government." By the close of the 1970s, there were 2,000 trade associations, with 50,000 employees, operating in the nation's capital.

The registration of corporate lobbyists increased from 175 in 1971 to almost 2,500 in 1982, and the number of corporate political action committees increased from 300 in 1976 to more than 1,200 by 1985.

Implementing Powell's instruction to "establish the staffs of eminent scholars, writers and speakers, who will do the thinking, the analysis, the writing and the speaking," the number of conservative, business-funded research foundations proliferated. In addition to the American Enterprise Institute, National Center for Public Policy Research, Hoover Institution, Freedom House, Tax Foundation and Foreign Policy Research Institute, and Hudson Institute which existed in 1971, the following major conservative institutions are among the hundreds that have been established since then: the Heritage Foundation; Cato Institute, Center for Strategic and International Studies; Pacific Legal Foundation; National Legal Center for the Public Interest; Acton Institute; Manhattan Institute for Policy Research; Pacific Research Institute; Foreign Policy in Focus; The Claremont Institute; American Foreign Policy Council; The Jamestown Foundation; Center for International Private Enterprise; National Center for Policy Analysis; Employment Policies Institute; The Heartland Institute; Allegheny Institute for Public Policy; George C. Marshall Institute; Goldwater Institute; and Center for Global Peace.

The success of the corporate-funded research foundations has been overwhelming. One study of the number of expert mainstream news media quotations from foundations found 48 percent to be from conservatives, 36 percent from centrists and only 16 percent from progressives.

Funded by billionaire Richard Mellon Scaife, heir to the Mellon fortune, the Federalist Society for Law and Public Policy Studies has grown to have 40,000 members. Its goal is the "reordering [of] priorities within the legal system to place a premium on individual liberty, traditional values, and the rule of law." U.S. Supreme Court Justice Antonin Scalia was a founder of the Society, and Chief Justice Roberts, Justice Alito and Justice Thomas are current members.

Established in 1972, the Business Roundtable is composed of the chief executives of America's largest and most powerful corporations. Employing more than 16 million people and booking annual revenues of more than $7.4 trillion, members have the power to talk to everyone holding office in the state and federal governments and to have their concerns dealt with.

The CEOs complained about President Carter's proposed tax bill, which closed loopholes and eliminated tax breaks for the wealthy. The bill was rewritten to benefit the very class of taxpayers Carter sought to regulate. They pushed through a new bankruptcy law which eased the requirements for corporate bankruptcy. It allowed corporate leaders to remain in control of bankrupt corporations, provided banks with the top priority for repayment, and left employees with the least rights. Finally, by passing legislation establishing "401(k)" retirement savings plans, Congress gave corporations the ability to eliminate their support of employee retirements.

One of the most successful strategies was the conversion of primarily Caucasian, blue-collar workers and their families— who were conservative in their support of the military and in opposition to racial integration and school busing—from the Democratic Party to the Republican Party. Referred to by Nixon as the Silent Majority and by Christian evangelists as the Moral Majority, they were encouraged by the language of free enterprise, populism, religion, and family values to oppose racial, sexual, social, and *economic* equality. The campaign successfully brainwashed millions of working people and small business owners to act and vote against their own economic interests.

Proclaiming a New Right, Ronald Reagan ran against President Carter in 1980. Reagan's support came from a coalition of corporate and wealthy elites, former Southern Democrats, hard-hat workers, and Christian evangelicals. He promised to end "the long, liberal experiment that began in the 1930s."

President Carter was weakened during the campaign by the continuing diplomatic hostage crisis in Iran. His attempts to extract the hostages failed and diplomatic negotiations were fruitless.

Serious allegations have been made that members of the Ronald Reagan election team, specifically William Casey (who would become the Director of the Central Intelligence Agency) and George H. W. Bush (who became Vice President), had contacts with the Iranian government during the campaign. Allegedly, the promise was made that, if the hostages were treated well and released as a gift to President Reagan, the Republicans would help Iran militarily.

Whether the allegations are true or not, these facts are: Iran broke off negotiations with Carter's officials and did not release the hostages until minutes after Ronald Reagan took the presidential oath of office on January 20, 1981; and acting through Israel, the Reagan administration began to sell large amounts of vital military equipment to Iran and to use the proceeds from the deal to fund the Nicaraguan Contra rebels in violation of U.S. law. If there was in fact a *quid pro quo* connection between these events, President Reagan took his oath under a cloud of treason.

Most political scientists believe the period of the Fifth Party System ended with the realignment of voters leading to the election of Ronald Reagan.

As President Reagan set about to dismantle the American Dream on behalf of his corporate sponsors, the harm he caused to the people who elected him is beyond calculation, but he was certainly the best political investment ever made by Corporate America.

The Creed of Greed

In what he called the "virtuous circle of growth," Henry Ford voluntarily raised the salary of his assembly line workers—so they would be able to buy the cars they manufactured. Later, Frank Abrams, the head of Standard Oil of New Jersey, advocated stakeholder capitalism, in which corporations balanced the needs of workers, shareholders, customers, and the public. Job security and employee contentment were indicators of a company's health.

University of Chicago professor Milton Friedman, the guru of the New Economy, had a different and far more selfish corporate philosophy. He said, "Few trends could so thoroughly undermine the very foundations of our free society as the acceptance by corporate officials of a social responsibility other than to make as much money for their stockholders as possible."

The original justification for corporations—they served a public purpose *and* limited the liability of their investors—became twisted by Friedman and his disciples. In the New Economy, the assets of a corporation are *owned* by its shareholders and are held in trust for their benefit by the company executives. The executives have a fiduciary duty to increase the value of the company stock at all costs. In this scenario, greed is not only good, it is the preeminent responsibility of corporate management.

Moreover, since it is the duty of company officers to earn the greatest return possible on shareholder's investments, it is in the interest of the shareholders that the officers also hold a stake in the company. That way, the more the officers earn for themselves, the more they earn for all shareholders. Thus, the stock compensation plan was born, and corporations came to serve, not the public, not the shareholders, but the officers who run the companies.

As corporations, financial institutions, their officers, and the wealthy elite became more powerful and extended their control over the political process, they found a perfect candidate to hire as their front man with the American people.

Ronald Reagan, Corporate Pitchman

With an Irish salesman and yarn spinner for a father, Ronald Reagan was a born showman. Reagan's good looks and gift of gab smoothed his way from college cheerleader, to radio announcer, and to Hollywood actor by the time he was 26 years old. He served out World War II in an army motion picture unit in Los Angeles, where he was promoted to Captain for his public relations achievements. Allegedly, he later showed a film of the liberation of Auschwitz to the Israeli foreign minister, saying he had filmed the footage himself.

Costarring in "B" movies with a chimpanzee, Reagan became active in the Screen Actors Guild and was its president during the McCarthy era. He served as an FBI informant, revealed the names of those he suspected of being communists or sympathizers, and testified before the House Un-American Activities Committee.

When the movie producers stopped calling and his dance routine on the Las Vegas strip flopped, Reagan became the spokesman for the General Electric corporation in its sponsorship of a series of weekly television dramas. As a part of GE's "citizen education" campaign to promote a "better business environment," Reagan's television contract also required him to tour GE factories and make conservative, pro-business, low tax, and anti-union speeches to the officers and employees.

Originally a Democrat, who had supported President Truman, Reagan joined the Republican Party and shifted his support to Eisenhower and Nixon. He opposed civil rights legislation in the 1960s saying, "If an individual wants to discriminate against Negroes or others in selling or renting his house, it's his right to do so." He also opposed Medicare, believing it meant the end of freedom in America and that "we will awake and find we have socialism."

Speaking on behalf of Barry Goldwater's presidential campaign in 1961, Reagan said:

> You and I are told we must choose between a left or right, but I suggest there is no such thing as a left or right. There is only up or down. Up to man's age-old dream—the maximum of individual freedom consistent with order—or down to the ant heap of totalitarianism.

Goldwater's "Millionaire Backers" in California loved Reagan's performance and ran him for governor in 1966 on a platform to clean up the university campuses and "to get the welfare bums back to work." As governor, Reagan dispatched the California Highway Patrol to put down anti-war protests at UC Berkeley's

Peace Park—in which shotguns were indiscriminately used on students. He said, "Once the dogs of war have been unleashed, you must expect things will happen." He activated the National Guard to occupy the city of Berkeley for two weeks, saying, "If it takes a bloodbath, let's get it over with."

Reagan was reelected in 1970, and used his governorship as a platform for a run on the presidency in 1976 against Republican moderate President Gerald Ford. He was endorsed by the American Conservative Union, but lost to Ford in the primaries. Ford was nominated, but was defeated by Jimmy Carter.

Four years later, Reagan's business backers used a loophole in the campaign financing law to funnel millions of dollars in soft money into another run for the presidency. This pioneer effort to move money from corporations to presidential candidates established a precedent for future campaigns.

Reagan won the 1980 election, and in an adroit switch of responsibility, Reagan claimed that government, rather than business, was the problem. He made a marriage of political convenience with British Prime Minister Margaret Thatcher, and in a joint celebration of economic freedom, they proclaimed that getting rich through business capitalism was the solution for the world's problems, and governments should get out of the way.

The new Secretaries of State, Defense, and Treasury came from corporate and financial backgrounds, and regulatory agencies were staffed with corporate executives having a clear conflict of interest in the matters regulated. Corporations that encountered regulatory problems were encouraged to bring their concerns directly to the White House, which appointed the regulators and set their budgets. Staff and budgets were immediately cut at many agencies, including the Food and Drug Administration, the Occupational Safety and Hazard

Administration, the Mine Safety and Health Administration, the Consumer Product Safety Commission and the Environmental Protection Agency.

In a reverse twist, regulations were imposed which limited corporate liability and protected corporations from competition. These federal regulations were written and proposed by the industries to be regulated and preempted attempts by the states to impose more effective regulations.

Stage-managed by an astute staff of political directors and producers, the White House became a showcase for Corporate America and the imperial presidency, and Reagan was the master performer. He was closely scripted, and his ad libs and one-liners were kept to a minimum. Presidential policies were reduced to advertising slogans, with carefully crafted punch lines delivered by Reagan from his cue cards.

The Reagan administration perfected the concept of perception management to avoid telling the truth to the public. The People's perceptions were managed through the slick use of propaganda. Depending on the needs of the moment, fears were incited to gain support for military programs contrary to the public interest, or public outrage was turned aside or redirected to other more vulnerable targets, such as immigrants or minorities.

The mining of harbors and the encouragement of human rights violations in Nicaragua by the United States was condemned by the International Court of Justice. As a cover up, right-wing media executives were recruited to financially support and participate in a CIA propaganda campaign to manipulate the opinion of Americans. Reagan referred to the Contra terrorists as "the moral equivalent of our founding fathers."

The ability to spin outcomes became as important as the issues themselves. A prime example was Reagan's meeting with Mikhail Gorbachev in 1986 to discuss nuclear arms control. It was a complete failure; however, the meeting was "spun" as Reagan's "finest hour," as he made a far-reaching arms control proposal. Gorbachev's refusal to even consider the proposal was ignored, and nobody noticed.

Merrill Lynch CEO Donald Regan was Reagan's treasury secretary, before becoming his Chief of Staff in 1985. Regan became the Prime Minister of Reagan's Imperial Presidency, before he was forced to resign over the Iran/Contra scandal. Regan later wrote, "Virtually every major move and decision the Reagans made during my time as White House Chief of Staff was cleared in advance with . . . horoscopes to make certain the planets were in a favorable alignment for the enterprise."

America became a consumer nation, and its people were trained by commercial advertising to buy the political products being peddled by Big Business and Wall Street. Workers, small business owners, and the middle class turned their backs on the poor and disadvantaged, and acquiesced in the realignment of government programs from the People to the corporations and wealthy elite. The size of the government was not reduced, but its protection was redirected from the weak to the strong.

More in line with Hitler's slogan over the entrance to Auschwitz, *Arbeit macht frei* (work will set you free), than with Roosevelt's Four Freedoms, Reagan called for: "The freedom to work. The freedom to enjoy the fruits of one's labor. The freedom to own and control one's property. The freedom to participate in a free market." These were later combined into the more pithy Freedom of Enterprise.

The real American Dream was replaced with an illusionary American Dream from the world of advertising. The freedoms promised by Roosevelt, and enjoyed by the common people, were transformed into the shackles of economic slavery for most American workers and small business owners by Ronald Reagan, the corporate huckster. Ordinary people were denied the opportunity and freedom to participate in Reagan's marketplace of privileged enterprise—which increasingly became the economic Las Vegas and Atlantic City of the rich and corporate elite.

Aided by a compliant and consolidated, corporate-controlled media, the Reagan administration focused its attack on the labor movement and taxes. Reagan invoked a national emergency when the union of federal air traffic controllers went on strike—he fired 11,345 striking workers and banned them from the federal civil service for life.

To the extent freedom to participate in the enterprise of a free market extends to both labor and capital, Ronald Reagan placed the federal government's thumb on the capital side of the scales of freedom. Thereafter, private employers were empowered and less constrained to fire and replace striking workers, and the political power and influence of organized labor began a steady decline.

Reagan's first treasury secretary, Paul O'Neill, believed corporations should be exempt from all income taxes and that Social Security and Medicare should be abolished. He said, "able-bodied adults should save enough on a regular basis so that they can provide for their own retirement, and, for that matter, health and medical needs."

The Reagan administration abandoned the conservative economic principle of a balanced budget and reduced the top marginal tax rate for wealthy individuals from 70 to 50 percent. At the same time, social security taxes on workers' payrolls were increased, while the capital gains rate on unearned income from wealth was decreased.

The corporate tax rate, which had been 32 percent in the 1950s, was cut to 12.5 percent. Many giant corporations, including General Electric (Reagan's former boss), would go years without having to pay taxes.

The economic theory of Reaganomics was that a reduction in tax income would stimulate the economy, resulting in an expansion of the tax base sufficient to make up for the loss in revenue. Moreover, it was claimed that some of the increased income of the wealthy resulting from their lower taxes would trickle down to poor people—who were on their own.

Unable to cut entitlement programs such as Social Security and Medicare, the Reagan administration froze minimum wages and reduced the budgets of state Medicaid, local government and community assistance, housing, food stamps, unemployment insurance, and anti-poverty programs.

While cutting domestic spending, Reagan vastly increased military spending, revived the B-1 bomber program eliminated by Carter, produced a new multiple-warhead ballistic missile and deployed nuclear-capable missiles in Germany. He launched the Strategic Defense Initiative (Star Wars) to produce a worthless, $30 billion, ground- and space-based anti-ballistic missile system that was never completed. Undertaken to benefit the military-industrial complex, these wasteful programs were an unjustified expense and tax burden on the American people, in light of fact the Soviet Union was in the final stage of political, economic, and social collapse.

Reagan announced a new War on Drugs in 1982, which included a major increase in funding and mandatory sentences for drug offenses. His wife, Nancy, promoted a "just say no to drugs and alcohol" campaign aimed at students. The number of young people, particularly minorities, convicted of drug offenses and sentenced to prison began to rise to epidemic proportions.

The Reagan administration reversed years of grass-roots efforts leading to effective regulations by the Federal Communications Commission (FCC) to limit television advertising directed at children and to improve the quality and diversification of child-oriented programming.

The Reagan-appointed FCC Commission also repealed the Fairness Doctrine, which had required broadcasters to provide a balance of political opinion in their programming. With its repeal and the subsequent corporate consolidation of radio and television outlets, the public became exposed to a one-sided barrage of conservative political messaging.

Initially, taxes on income were only collected from the wealthy, and when the tax was implemented by Constitutional amendment in 1913, less than one percent of the population paid it. As the tax was expanded to all incomes, percentage brackets were based on the ability to pay, with the greatest incomes paying the highest percentage.

The top bracket of personal federal income taxes, which was 92 percent under President Eisenhower and 77 percent under President Kennedy, dropped to 50 percent under President Reagan. The maximum has continued to be reduced to the present top bracket of 39.6 percent.

As the Reagan budgets for the military and homeland defense continued to grow, the burden of taxation increasingly shifted from the wealthy to the middle and working classes, and real incomes declined. By every metric, the rich got richer, and workers and small business owners became poorer.

Here are the bottom-line facts. President Reagan did not reduce the size of government; overall federal employment rose from 4.9 million in 1981 to 5.3 million in 1989. He did not reduce the federal budget; it was $678 billion when he took office and it was $1.1 trillion when he left. He did not reduce the federal deficit; it was increased from $79 billion to $155 billion under his administration. Finally, the national debt tripled from $997 billion to $2.85 trillion during the Reagan years.

The sales pitch that high taxes are a drag on the economy, while low taxes stimulate it, caused the personal financial status of most Americans to suffer. Well-paying jobs disappeared, the prices of necessities increased, and the middle-class faded away, along with the American Dream. The power of Reagan's spin machine to distort reality is demonstrated by how easily these dismal failures were rewritten into a script of President Reagan as a great leader.

Instead of acknowledging the abuses of his administration and learning from its failures, there has been a concerted effort to deify Reagan. Repeatedly, there have been failed congressional attempts to substitute Reagan's image for Franklin Roosevelt on dime coins, Alexander Hamilton on $10 bills, Andrew Jackson on $20 bills, and Ulysses Grant on $50 bills. The Ronald Reagan Legacy Project has the announced goal of naming a landmark for him in every county in the United States. Success of the project can be observed firsthand as one travels through the communities of America, made destitute, impoverished, and disheartened by those who created and manipulated the political hologram of Ronald Reagan, the greatest show in Washington.

Consolidation of the Corporate State

Much of what we take for granted in the modern society we live in would be impossible without corporations. Supermarkets filled with great varieties of fresh produce and selections of ready-to-cook foods, big-box stores with appliances, clothing, and electronic devices, the movies we attend, and the television and videos we watch would not be possible without corporations to plan and operate these enterprises. Nor would we have the ability to travel by air anywhere in the world within a matter of days, and be connected with our smartphones upon arrival. We would not be able to type these words on a computer, send them over the Internet and read them on a display monitor.

Corporations are as much a part of our lives as our places of worship, the schools our children attend, our governments and the wars they fight. At their present rate of expansion, however, corporations are increasingly taking on these functions as well.

Indeed, it is the ability of corporations to plan, finance, organize, and manage large and complex projects that originally permitted their creation for the public good. They have, however, mutated into cancerous entities that threaten the public they were intended to serve, and they are unaccountable, even to their own shareholders.

The evaluation of corporations shifted from the quality of the goods and services they provided and the dividends they paid, to how much their stocks are valued by Wall Street. Chief Executive Officers (CEOs) are ranked by how much the price of their company's stock increases during their management. As CEOs receive ever greater bonuses, stock options and salaries, they become increasingly disconnected from their workers.

In the 1970s, CEOs earned approximately 40 times that of their average worker. Today S&P 500 CEOs earn an average of $15.2 million annually, or more than 331 times their average employee. In corporations employing large numbers of part-time workers, such as Wal-Mart and McDonald's, the multiple is more than 500 times the average. These executives earn more in one hour than their workers do in a year.

As private sector union membership fell from 27 percent in the 1970s to less than seven percent today, American CEOs have achieved unrestrained power in the operation of their companies. Relying on compliant, inter-locking boards of directors, they are able to do whatever they deem necessary to drive up the price of their company's stock. Oftentimes, the action taken makes no other economic sense.

Historically, the fear of corporate trusts and industrial monopolies has been nonpartisan. Republican President Theodore Roosevelt was known as the "trustbuster" for his enforcement of the Sherman Antitrust Act. He warned:

> The fortunes amassed through corporate organization are now so large, and vest such power in those that wield them, as to make it a matter of necessity to give to the sovereign— that is, to the Government, which represents the people as a whole—some effective power of supervision over their corporate use. In order to ensure a healthy social and industrial life, every big corporation should be held responsible by, and be accountable to, some sovereign strong enough to control its conduct.

Theodore Roosevelt's cousin, Democratic President Franklin Roosevelt, agreed:

Throughout the nation, opportunity was limited by monopoly. Individual initiative was crushed in the cogs of a great machine. The field open for free business was more and more restricted. Private enterprise, indeed, became too private. It became privileged enterprise, not free enterprise.

Since the Reagan administration, the Securities and Exchange Commission has largely allowed corporations to self-regulate their mergers and hostile corporate takeovers. Attorney General William French Smith said, "Bigness in business is not necessarily badness. Efficient firms should not be hobbled under the guise of antitrust enforcement." The result has been a massive consolidation of industries and the creation of multi-industry conglomerates.

A typical leveraged buyout involves the borrowing of substantial funds to pay for an acquisition, followed by severe cost cutting, delayed investment in future productivity, and massive layoffs of employees to produce paper profits and increase share value. The resulting conglomerate is often purchased by a corporate raider, who then sells off the various parts previously assembled. The employees are without economic value in these machinations and are discarded in the process; customers are bewildered, and communities that have provided tax breaks and infrastructure for the corporations are devastated.

Rather than investing in capital facilities and new products—which would allow American corporations to compete with other countries—CEOs rely on accounting tricks and tax avoidance schemes to provide an illusion of profitability. The fiduciary duty to shareholders is replaced by self-interest, as the top executives of companies award themselves scandalous salaries, exercise stock options, and collect bonuses. Even when they fail, "golden parachutes" allow them to walk away with massive payoffs.

With reduced regulation and taxes, the failure of American companies to compete in the international markets is due to short-term profit-taking over long-term investments in employee training, plants, equipment and new products. More than anything else, personal greed, rather than strategic thinking, motivates corporate decision making.

By the time of the dot-com crash of 2000, American corporations were setting world records for size and mergers. Mobil Oil purchased Exxon, creating the world's largest company; Worldcom Incorporated took over MCI, becoming the largest telecommunications company; and AOL merged with Time Warner, making it the largest media company.

When the bubble burst, Worldcom, which had gobbled up 75 companies in five years, saw its paper profits turn into massive losses and its share price fall by 95 percent. The stock of Tyco International, which had acquired as many as 1,000 companies, fell by 60 percent. The original value of the AOL-Time Warner merger was $318 billion. By 2003, the company was valued at only $62 billion, with $26 billion in debt. Overall, the share value of the 50 most active merger companies dropped more than three times the Dow Jones Industrial Average.

Just as occurred during the Roaring Twenties, ordinary people had been enticed to invest in corporate stocks and bonds, and once again the hard-earned savings of millions of American workers and small business owners were wiped out.

The gross domestic product of a nation is the value of goods and services produced within a calendar year. The annual gross profits of a corporation is a measure of its total productivity.

Today, the largest 100 world economies by gross product include the major countries, such as the United States, but more than half of these top economies are corporations.

It is not that the U.S. government is without the means to control corporate merger madness—it is that the power of the government has been subverted to serve corporate interests, rather than to regulate them. Effectively, the Internal Revenue Service no longer forces major corporations and financial institutions to abide by the tax laws, and the Securities Exchange Commission and the Federal Trade Commission no longer regulate their activities.

The president of the United States earns $400,000 annually and is the highest paid federal civil servant. That's chump change to corporate executives, as even those at lower levels earn more than the president and members of Congress. Corporate executives have little respect for those who are elected by the American people to represent them. The caretakers of the public interest have become irrelevant to Corporate America, and its CEOs have become masters of all they survey.

World Corporate Government

The United States is not alone in coming under corporate control. Corporations operate internationally, and they have created a series of international banking and trade agreements that provide them with the power to dominate all of the world's governments.

World War II was coming to an end in July 1944, as representatives of 44 nations, bankers, and economists gathered at Bretton Woods, New Hampshire for the International Monetary and Financial Conference of the United and

Associated Nations. Three weeks of meetings resulted in the Bretton Woods Agreement, which was the outline for the International Monetary Fund (IMF), the World Bank and the General Agreement on Tariffs and Trade (GATT), which later became known as the World Trade Organization (WTO).

Fearing its great power, the last of these agreements, the GATT/WTO treaty, was not ratified by the U.S. Senate until near the end of the Clinton Administration in 1994. The World Trade Organization harmonizes the laws of all nations through the use of Dispute Resolution Panels, consisting of corporate attorneys, to review complaints by corporations against governmental organizations accusing them of unfairly restraining trade. National laws intended to protect consumers, workers, or the environment can be overturned by these panels that act in secret. Moreover, offending countries can be ordered to reimburse corporations for their lost profits.

The Philip Morris tobacco corporation is currently in litigation with the nations of Uruguay, Norway and Australia alleging their anti-smoking legislation devalues its cigarette trademarks and investments. The matter will be decided by binding arbitration before the International Center for Settlement of Investment Disputes.

In 1988, President H. W. Bush obtained Congressional approval of a new fast-track procedure to secure Senate ratification of trade agreements. These agreements, which can reach thousands of pages of highly complex terms and conditions, are negotiated in great secrecy by government trade representatives assisted by corporate consultants. They are then presented for ratification as a fait accompli during a very short period, with limited debate. Using fast track, President Clinton obtained approval of GATT/WTO in 1994.

Playing the same game, Clinton obtained ratification of the North American Free Trade Agreement (NAFTA), which had been negotiated during the Bush I administration. NAFTA is a complex, rules-based trade agreement between the United States, Canada, and Mexico. Following NAFTA, production was moved from the United States to Mexican factories just south of the border, where export goods are produced using low-wage workers. President Clinton claimed the agreement would create "American jobs, and good-paying American jobs." The AFL-CIO has documented the transfer of 700,000 of these well-paying American jobs to Mexico.

Two major trade agreements are presently being negotiated in great secrecy. These are the Trans-Pacific Partnership, which includes the United States and 11 other Asia-Pacific Rim nations, and the Transatlantic Trade and Investment Partnership between the European Union and the United States. If ratified, the combination of these trade agreements will govern almost all of the world's economic output. Rather than promoting free trade and competition for the benefit of consumers, the agreements will provide unregulated protection of corporate interests.

On May 14, 2015, the U.S. Senate, following an outpouring of corporate campaign contributions to the "fence sitters" passed Trade Promotion Authority, commonly known as fast tracking, allowing President Obama to rush the Trans-Pacific Partnership through Congress.

Inclusion of investor-state dispute settlements in these trade agreements creates a form of corporate sovereignty that supersedes the integrity of nation states. The deliberately vague language of these agreements leaves it up to the corporate arbitrators to decide whether national legislation or regulations "expropriate" foreign investments.

Under the Supremacy Clause of the Constitution, federal law and treaties are the Supreme Law of the Land. Such treaties, including these new trade agreements, are binding on all judges, "anything in the constitution or laws of any state to the contrary notwithstanding."

The power of international agreements to replace both the legislative and judicial functions of the U.S. government brings into question whether the people's consent to be governed continues to be valid. The Constitution states, "The United States shall guarantee to every State in this Union a Republican Form of Government." Can a government that is no longer controlled by the vote of the people be a republic?

All of these international financial and trade agreements restrict the ability of the United States to regulate matters concerning its own society in any way that violates free trade, including the taxing of corporations. The agreements create a world economic government, and that government is controlled by corporations, for the benefit of corporations. The people have value only as workers and consumers.

Globalization has contributed to the growing inequality in the worldwide distribution of wealth. An Oxfam report issued in January 2015 announced that the richest 80 people in the world have more wealth than the bottom 3,500,000,000 people. By next year, the wealthiest one percent will own more than the remaining 99 percent of the entire world population.

The Corporate Media
Throughout the history of the United States, a free and independent press has been considered a fourth branch of government. As a "fourth estate," it has served as a check on the power

of the executive, legislative, and judicial branches. Although the news media retains the freedom of the press granted by the First Amendment, it is no longer effective as an impartial monitor of government operations.

Today, six corporate conglomerates control 90 percent of what Americans read, watch, or listen to: CBS, Comcast, Disney, News-Corp, Time Warner and Viacom. These corporations have a monopoly over television and radio stations and their programming, control television and internet cables, and produce a majority of American movies and videos. Their revenues run to hundreds of billions of dollars each year, and their economic and political power is overwhelming.

The media giants not only dictate the kind of programming Americans are exposed to, but they also direct the political reporting and editorial positions of their news outlets. Equally important, they have the power to refuse advertising and coverage of issues they oppose—particularly any matter that challenges corporate power. The corporate bias affects the quality and quantity of reporting on political, economic, and environmental issues.

Accustomed to receiving an endless stream of one-way communications from radio and television, American consumers have become very accepting of the information they receive from the mainstream media and the picture it paints of life in America. As Adolf Hitler said, "Through clever and constant application of propaganda, people can be made to see paradise as hell, and also the other way round, to consider the most wretched sort of life as paradise."

Given the inordinate power of the mainstream media to distort facts and manipulate opinions, skeptical people are turning to the Internet, social media and other digital outlets for the truth. Online bloggers and websites, such as WikiLeaks, are increasingly considered by many to be the "fifth estate" sentinel of individual rights and a check on the power of corporate government.

The Economic Casino

Compulsive gambling, like alcoholism and drug addiction, is considered to be a human disease because it ultimately drives individuals and their families to destitution and ruin. Today, the disease has infected the world economic system, which is based more on reckless gambling, than on the rational provision and allocation of financial services.

The casino in which gambling takes place is the worldwide financial services industry—the banks are the bookies, complex financial instruments are the markers, and ordinary depositors and investors are the suckers. Gaming rooms at the casino are named for corporations, banks, and insurance companies.

Corporations are the oldest American businesses still operating. These include CIGNA insurance company (1792), Jim Beam distillery (1795), DuPont chemicals (1802) and Colgate consumer products (1806). The births of corporations, such as these, are conceived by state and federal statutes and nourished by shareholder investment. Corporations issue stocks and bonds, which are bought and sold in market places, such as the New York Stock Exchange on Wall Street, using investment banks and brokerages to place and hold the bets.

Corporations can borrow money, purchase property, enter into contracts, employ humans, declare bankruptcy, and commit crimes. Unlike mere humans, however, corporations can avoid prison, accumulate unlimited wealth, and enjoy everlasting life.

Because of their immense potential power, corporations are only allowed to exist under two legal conditions: limited liability and public service.

Corporations limit the liability of an investor to the amount of the investment. If someone buys $100 worth of corporate stocks, that $100 is all the investor stands to lose, no matter what happens. Just like governments, corporations can also issue bonds, which are purchased by investors and repaid over time at a fixed rate of interest. Stocks and bonds are liquid—if they can be bought, sold, or traded in a marketplace.

Ideally, corporations are only allowed to exist if they serve the public good and not some illegal purpose. Unfortunately, many corporations have come to engage in conduct that is harmful to the public. Taking on a godlike status, corporations are increasingly finding ways to avoid the responsibilities imposed by their charters, including paying taxes and benefiting the public.

Playing the corporate stock and bond market is a gamble and, depending on market conditions and the quality of their management, some corporations succeed and others fail. Some investors win and some lose, and the difference often depends on inside information that is not available to ordinary investors.

Banks are also created for gambling. Depositors gamble that the bank will not fail when they put money into a bank account, and banks gamble on repayment when they loan money. Commercial banks are supposed to operate very conservatively—in order to minimize the risk of default and to pay a guaranteed rate of interest on deposits. Investment banks, however, underwrite and finance the purchase and sale of corporate stocks and bonds, in which both the risks and the return on investments are greater.

Banks charge interest, fees and commissions every time money moves through their accounts, and their profits depend on how quickly the money moves and the amount of risk the movement entails.

Banks do not keep all of the funds they have on deposit in their vaults. Trusting that all of their depositors will not demand a return of their money at the same time, banks keep only a small fraction of deposits on hand. Fractional-reserve banking allows banks to use the balance of the deposits to loan money for fixed rates of interest and to make more risky investments in order to earn greater returns. As the money is loaned and spent, it grows with each redeposit in banks. Assuming a 20 percent fractional reserve, an initial deposit of $100, can quickly create $400, as the liquid $80 flows and grows with each redeposit in the banking system.

To guard against a run on individual banks, central banks have been established in most countries to establish the minimum reserve limits for individual banks and to loan them money to meet unexpected demands. The first central bank of the United States was established by Alexander Hamilton.

Andrew Jackson opposed central banking and the political power it conferred on those who operated the bank. He said:

> In this point of the case the question is distinctly presented whether the people of the United States are to govern through representatives chosen by their unbiased suffrages or whether the money and power of a great corporation are to be secretly exerted to influence their judgment and control their decisions.

Jackson removed all federal funds from the Second Bank of the United States, causing it to cease operations in 1833. Thereafter, the United States was without a central bank for 80 years, as it went through at least four major financial panics and depressions.

The last of these began in 1893 when the New York stock market crashed. More than 16,000 businesses, including 500 banks and 150 railroads failed during the following four-year depression. One in six workers lost their jobs, and thousands marched in "Coxey's Army" on Washington, DC to demand government public works projects to provide employment.

In 1910, the most powerful politician in the country was Republican Senator Nelson Aldrich from Rhode Island, who was the chairman of the Senate Finance Committee. He invited a group of bankers to a private island resort in Georgia to draft, secretly, legislation incorporating a central bank for bankers.

The Federal Reserve Act of 1913 created the Federal Reserve System. The "Fed" consists of 12 regional reserve banks owned by the member banks in each region. The System is overseen by a Board of Governors, and the Chair of the Board is appointed by the president, subject to Senate confirmation.

The United States maintains the taxes it collects from the public in the Federal Reserve, which redeems savings bonds and treasury instruments issued by the government. The Fed also distributes and controls the currency and coins printed and minted by the U.S. Treasury—although money increasingly consists of digital entries in computerized accounts. The System is empowered to expand or contract the supply of money to meet changing economic conditions.

Member banks must deposit their cash reserves in the Federal Reserve, which sets the interest rate on interbank loan of reserve funds—whereby banks loan their excess deposits to each other overnight to maintain required minimum balances— and the discount rate for the Fed's direct lending to member banks. The Fed supervises the check-clearing and interbank lending systems, and it is the lender of last resort to struggling banks.

The Federal Reserve does not receive government financing or pay taxes, and it turns over its excess profits to the government.

Insurance is another financial gamble, with an insurance company betting on how long before you die, your house burns down, or you have a traffic accident. You hope none of these events occur, but you pay premiums into an insurance fund gambling the agreed upon amount will be paid out—if and when the tragedy occurs. Insurance companies invest their reserve funds gambling they will increase their profits.

Corporations, banks, and insurance companies are all motivated by greed and the desire to get the most for the least. As long as all parties are economically sophisticated, market forces can determine the winners and the losers. When, however, corporate stock or other financial instruments are offered for sale to the general public, there is a great risk that ordinary investors will be fraudulently taken advantage of.

The risks to the public were demonstrated during the stock market boom of the 1920s. Rising net profits of America's major corporations fueled a frenzy of stock speculation by hundreds of thousands of ordinary investors. Many purchased stocks "on margin" by borrowing 90 percent of the purchase price with a 10 percent down payment. By August 1929, more money was on loan to purchase stocks than there was in circulation.

Everything was fine as long as the value of stocks continued to rise, but when the market crashed in October 1929, and the value of stocks plummeted, the margins were "called" by brokers. The investment of everyone who could not immediately produce sufficient cash to make up the difference in the value of the depreciated stock and what was owed, was wiped out. As defaults multiplied, depositors lost confidence in banks and began to withdraw their money. Banks began to cease operations and lock their doors, and depositors who didn't make it in time were left empty handed.

Within days, billions of dollars in paper wealth disappeared, and thousands of ordinary people lost their investments and life savings. A great economic depression descended upon the world—half of America's banks failed, a third of its workers became unemployed, and there was insufficient money left in the economy to finance a recovery.

Banks called in their defaulting loans and stopped lending; businesses were unable to borrow and maintain operations; people liquidated their assets to pay off their debts; prices fell and the value of money rose. The wealth of those who were rich, and had money reserves, sharply increased. The rich got richer, while the rest of America slumped into abject poverty.

Congress responded to the gambling conditions that caused the crash of the stock market with the Banking Act of 1933. The Act imposed banking reforms, including the Federal Deposit Insurance Corporation (FDIC), which insures deposits in member banks of the Federal Reserve.

The Banking Act, also known as the Glass-Steagall Act, more specifically refers to four primary provisions which separated commercial banking and insurance companies (which have fiduciary duties to invest wisely) from investment banks and securities firms (which are allowed to be more speculative). In addition, restrictions were imposed on the ability of commercial banks to engage in speculation in stocks, commodities, or real estate, or to pay interest on checking accounts. Large banks were not allowed to open branch banks in states where they were not chartered.

Small "thrift," or savings and loan, institutions (S&Ls) primarily accepted personal savings deposits and offered small home construction loans for the working and middle classes. S&Ls were not included in the Banking Act; however, Congress created the Federal Savings and Loan Insurance Corporation (FSLIC) in 1934 to insure their deposits.

Following World War II and the postwar home construction boom, S&Ls became more openly competitive with commercial banks. To entice deposits, they offered higher rates of interest on savings accounts than commercial banks. Congress imposed interest rate limits for both S&Ls and commercial banks in 1966.

To attract business, S&Ls created interest-bearing checking accounts and alternatives to standard mortgages. A rise in interest rates and inflation during the 1970s challenged the financial health of S&Ls, and they lobbied for permission to engage in more profitable operations that posed greater risks.

Congress responded with legislation in 1980 and 1982 that deregulated the industry. The lending authority of S&Ls was extended, and they were empowered to offer adjustable-rate mortgages. Emphasis on personal savings and home ownership was reduced, along with supervisory oversight. S&Ls were allowed new investment options, including commercial real estate, consumer loans, and issuance of credit cards.

The S&L industry quickly became infamous for massive fraud and insider trading, as executives took advantage of deregulation to accept large institutional brokered deposits and to make reckless business investments. There was a tsunami of failures by S&Ls in what became known as the Savings and Loan Crisis.

Between 1986 and 1989, the FSLIC dealt with almost 300 failed S&Ls with assets of $125 billion. The FSLIC became hopelessly insolvent and was abolished in 1989. Its assets and liabilities were transferred to the FSLIC Resolution Fund, and its deposit insurance responsibility was transferred to the commercial bank FDIC. The Resolution Trust Corporation had to "resolve" an additional 750 S&Ls. Altogether, one-third of all S&Ls failed. More than $160 billion was lost during the crisis, and *the cost to taxpayers* was between $124 and $132 billion.

The fact that the government stepped in and bailed out the S&L industry was not lost on the CEOs of other financial institutions, as they lobbied for deregulation of their activities allowing them engage in speculative money-making schemes. Their ally was Donald T. Regan, the former chairman of the Merrill Lynch brokerage firm, who was Ronald Reagan's treasury secretary. Regan's goal was to "allow all depository institutions to make the same type of loans in whatever amount they see fit."

The dream of enormous profits was driving financial institutions to create and market new forms of investment-grade securities to satisfy the demands of the international financial system. Financiers envisioned a new economic order no longer based on the slow, but sure, production of wealth through invention, manufacturing, and export. Instead, wealth could be instantly created through the use of paper and computers, without regard for risk or fraud.

A new multisyllabic word—securitization—was added to the financial vocabulary. It is the pooling of various kinds of contractual debt, such as mortgages, and selling the consolidated debt as a more liquid, or salable, security, such as bonds and mortgage-based securities. By creating these new instruments, that could be more easily traded in the financial markets, value would be added with each transaction, and fees and commissions could be collected by the financial institutions on every deal. Moreover, because of their superior knowledge and insider information, the institutions could buy and sell the new instruments on their own behalf, using their customer's deposits.

High profits carry high risks, and the unrestrained creativity of the new economic order included ways for corporations to keep the profits and avoid jeopardy, by shifting the risks to their customers and the government. Paper value became more important than products, and the stock value of corporations became paramount to the quality of the goods and services they produced.

The financial industry was nonpartisan when it invested in the political parties and their candidates. In return, the industry demanded bipartisan support of its high-risk gambling schemes. While Congress did not *legislatively* deregulate financial institutions until the later Clinton administration, the Reagan and Bush I administrations *de facto* deregulated the industry by curtailing regulatory actions.

Responding to the electoral successes of Ronald Reagan and the Republican Party in the 1980s, some Democrats became convinced their party had to move to the center—if it were to retain political relevance. They formed the Democratic Leadership Council in 1985 to advocate the Third Way, which was a series of centralist policies. Sounding like moderate Republicans, who are socially progressive and economically conservative, the Third Way team crossed over the center into right field, as it wholeheartedly adopted the neoliberal economic philosophy of Milton Friedman.

The New Democrats favored deregulation of the economy to allow Big Business—rather than the government—to solve unemployment problems, and for market incentives to facilitate the trickle of wealth from the top to the bottom. Arkansas governor Bill Clinton was a founding member of the Council and served as its chairman. U.S. Senators Al Gore and Joseph Biden were also active in Council affairs.

The rise of the neoliberals and the New Democrats clearly establish that a Sixth Party System has come into existence. The two major parties have become aligned in their shared fealty to corporate power and on most political and economic matters of major importance.

A self-described New Democrat, Governor Clinton ran for president in 1992. His platform called for welfare reform, a middle-class tax cut, an increase in the upper tax rate, and a balanced budget. He followed through after his election with the Omnibus Budget Reconciliation Act of 1993 and the earned income tax credit.

With wholehearted Republican support, Clinton signed the North American Free Trade Agreement, which commenced the export of American jobs; the Defense of Marriage Act, which allowed states to refuse to recognize gay marriages performed in other states; the Illegal Immigration Reform and Immigrant Responsibility Act, which clamped down on illegal immigration; and the Personal Responsibility and Work Opportunity Reconciliation Act of 1996, which pushed welfare down to the states and forced poor single women with children to work or lose benefits.

President Clinton made a series of critical appointments to key financial regulatory positions. To "satisfy the bond market," Clinton twice reappointed Alan Greenspan as Chairman of the Federal Reserve System. Greenspan, a literal disciple of conservative philosopher Ayn Rand and a fervent believer in free market and monetarist principles, was originally appointed by President Reagan. Robert Rubin (who had spent 26 years at the investment banking firm of Goldman Sachs and was its co-chairman) was appointed Secretary of the Treasury, and his acolyte, Lawrence Summers, became his deputy. (Summers would later replace Rubin as Clinton's treasury secretary.)

With these appointments, the fox was placed in charge of the chicken coop, and the Reagan Era corporate goals were advanced to previously unachievable levels. The assault on financial regulation took place on several fronts.

The federal loan mortgage corporations commonly known as Fannie Mae and Freddie Mac were created by federal statute to purchase bank mortgages in support of home ownership. The process allows banks to quickly sell mortgages and to use the receipts for additional home loans. The banks earn money from higher fees and "points," instead of collecting low levels of interest over the long term of the mortgages.

Ninety percent of the loans purchased by the federal loan mortgage corporations in 1990 were solid prime loans, with substantial down payments and proven credit capacity. Relying on a provision in the 1977 Community Reinvestment Act, which required banks to meet local credit needs, the Clinton administration pressured banks to make subprime loans.

The Housing and Community Development Act of 1992 forced Fannie Mae and Freddie Mac to increase their purchase of higher risk "affordable-housing" mortgage loans to 30 percent. The proportion was raised to 40 percent in 1996, 42 percent in 1997 and 50 percent in 2000. To meet these goals, the federal loan mortgage corporations encouraged banks and S&Ls to relax lending standards.

The Destruction of Freedom

In 1998, Citicorp, a bank holding company, merged with the insurance company, Travelers Group, to form Citigroup, which combined insurance, investment, and commercial banking services. This merger was in violation of the Glass-Steagall requirement that commercial and insurance activities be kept separate from investment banking.

In November 1999, Clinton signed the Financial Services Modernization Act of 1999, which legitimized the birth of Citigroup. The Act authorized the formation of gigantic banking corporations, such as Citigroup, Bank of America, and J.P. Morgan Chase. They were allowed to have commercial branches nationally and to buy and sell stocks, finance corporate mergers, and sell insurance.

In addition to the ordinary trade in corporate stocks and bonds, the financial markets also engaged in a more exotic form of gambling known as "futures." The concept of futures allows individuals and firms to gamble that the price of certain stocks or other variables will either rise or fall in the future. Most commonly, these variables include bonds, commodities, currencies, interest rates, and stocks. Gamblers do not have to actually buy or own the variables to play—they simply purchase an option to buy or sell at an agreed price for a period of time or at a future date. The option allows them to sell at a profit if they win, or they will have to buy at a loss, if they lose. Futures have been regulated by the Commodity Exchange Act ever since 1936.

Financial gamblers are always seeking ways to minimize their risks when gambling about unpredictable futures. To help cover their wagers, the financial services industry created an even riskier financial instrument, which produced even greater returns for the banks. "Derivatives" are contracts that allow someone who gambles on future variables to insure against loss. The value of a derivative "derives" from and is dependent on the fluctuating value of one or more underlying assets.

Derivatives can be used to bet against oneself. For example, a gambler can bet one million dollars that a particular event will take place, and then bet $800,000 that it will not take place. That way, the player "hedges" the bet, and the most that can be lost will be $200,000. A sophisticated gambler will have more wins than losses and can make enormous profits. In these transactions, nothing is produced. Hedge funds allow investors to place their money in the hands of successful gamblers to play with, and to share in the winnings.

Traded derivatives are so complex as to be inherently fraudulent. They are so complicated that even experienced financial professionals have difficulty understanding and explaining them to their customers. Business magnate Warren Buffett called them "financial weapons of mass destruction."

The final blow to financial sanity and responsibility was the Commodity Futures Modernization Act of 2000 (CFMA) that unleashed the market for derivatives and encouraged banks to become even more aggressive in mortgage investments. The Commodity Exchange Act of 1936 continued to regulate security futures; however, CFMA held that over-the-counter derivative transactions between sophisticated parties would not be regulated as futures.

Derivatives quickly joined stocks, bonds, and mortgages as the primary categories of financial instruments. Of these, derivatives are so speculative that they verge on criminal gambling, and CFMA specifically preempted the states from prosecuting the trading of derivatives as ordinary crimes.

The value of derivatives in play at any given time is measured in the trillions of dollars and the annual aggregate amounts to hundreds of trillions. The staggering amount of these transactions can be compared to the total 2013 U.S. federal budget of $3.8 trillion and the entire world Gross Domestic Product of $75 trillion.

One feature of derivatives tied together the entire stratagem of financial market deregulation. Since the underlying asset in a derivative does not have to be directly acquired, the ownership of the asset can be vicariously divided and allocated among various risk factors. Mortgage-backed securities were created to take advantage of this aspect. A group of illiquid mortgages are purchased and "securitized" into a liquid financial package that can be easily sold to investors. The security is sliced into "tranches," which offer different priorities in the repayment of the debts and which provide a hierarchy of risks. Investors can reduce the speculative risks through the purchase of derivatives.

All was well as long as home prices remained high and mortgage payments were made as scheduled, but when the mortgage-backed securities game was based on high-risk subprime mortgages and a real-estate bubble, it became a financial disaster waiting to happen.

Collectively, the epidemic of compulsive financial gambling resulting from the deregulation of the financial services industry can be compared to what happens when a group of young children eat a lot of cake and ice cream at a birthday party and begin to play afterwards. Experiencing a sugar high and the exuberance of childhood, they race around screaming, getting more and more out of control, until an adult has to come into the room and settle them down. The reckless gamblers who played in the financial markets during the first decade of the Twenty-first Century went bonkers with a money high, and there was no adult supervision to calm them down.

In the election of 2000, George W. Bush, a failed Texas businessman, whose primary qualification was his family name, was employed by Corporate America as its puppet and placed on stage by the Supreme Court. His administration did nothing to return sanity to the financial markets or to governmental fiscal responsibility.

When Bush's treasury secretary, Paul O'Neill, warned of a $500 billion budget deficit, in the absence of tax reform, he was fired and ultimately replaced by Henry Paulson, the former Chairman and CEO of Goldman Sachs.

The Bush II administration promoted an "ownership society" in which social security would be privatized, and workers' payroll taxes would be deposited into personal investment accounts in private banks. The accounts would be managed by the financial institutions, which would earn fees and commissions—as they gambled with the deposits.

Following the attacks on September 11, 2001, President Bush advised people to "Get down to Disney World in Florida. Take your families and enjoy life, the way we want it to be enjoyed." Americans took his advice and began to spend more and save less. Encouraged to buy more stuff, people signed up for more credit cards, refinanced their homes, and spent the equity. Household debt doubled from $7.4 trillion at the end of 2000 to $14.5 trillion—or 134 percent of disposable income—by 2008.

Mortgages were quickly sold by lending banks, bundled and sliced into mortgage-backed securities and resold to investors. The originating banks no longer had to worry about defaults, and lending standards fell by the wayside. Home loans became increasingly insane, with one-quarter of all loans becoming "interest only." Many were adjustable-rate mortgages requiring "no documentation" and subject only to automated underwriting.

The newly unregulated financial institutions, particularly investment banks and brokerages, issued massive amounts of bonds and invested the proceeds in mortgage-backed securities—gambling that homeowners would continue to meet their payments. Essentially, the banks borrowed at low rates of interest, in the expectation of receiving a higher rate of return from the mortgage-backed securities.

The financial services industry (21%) soared past manufacturing (12%) as the major component of the gross domestic product. Private debt ballooned from $11 to $48 trillion by 2007. America was no longer making things, but it was making money.

When the Federal Bureau of Investigation issued warnings about an epidemic of mortgage fraud and predatory lending, the Bush II administration invoked a Nineteenth Century banking law to preempt state predatory lending laws. The states were prohibited from protecting their people against the wild-eyed gambling of international bankers and government shills.

Responding to the dictates of banks and credit card companies, President Bush signed a new bankruptcy law which made it much more difficult for ordinary Americans to escape the burden of overwhelming debt. The law requires debtors to work out a repayment plan, rather than to have their debts discharged in bankruptcy and to receive a fresh start. Bush said, "too many people have abused the bankruptcy laws. If someone does not pay his or her debts, the rest of society ends up paying them."

U.S. home prices peaked in 2006 and began to decline. It became more difficult for home owners to refinance their adjustable-rate mortgages, as they began to reset at higher interest rates (and monthly payments). Mortgage delinquencies skyrocketed—the value of mortgage-backed securities began to fall, and the derivatives that guaranteed the securities were no longer such a great investment. Over the next three years, the financial markets came close to collapsing, causing massive suffering throughout the world economy.

The United States entered the longest recession it had experienced since the Great Depression. The stock market lost half of its value and housing prices fell nearly 30 percent. Six percent of the U.S. workforce, or almost nine million workers, lost their jobs and the Gross Domestic Product dropped by 40 percent.

During 2008, the investment banks, who had been the biggest gamblers, went bust. Lehman Brothers declared bankruptcy. Bear Stearns was sold to JP Morgan Chase; Merrill Lynch was snapped up by the Bank of America; and Wachovia was absorbed by Wells Fargo. Morgan Stanley and Goldman Sachs became commercial banks, so their wealthy customers could receive FDIC protection of the $56 billion of investment funds the banks had on deposit.

Washington Mutual, the nation's largest S&L, failed and was bought by JP Morgan Chase.

The Federal Reserve provided an $85 billion secured line of credit to the American International Group (AIG), the world's largest insurance company, which had insured derivatives against default and personally invested, heavily, in mortgage-backed securities.

The government imposed a conservatorship on Fannie Mae and Freddie Mack and pledged $200 billion in new capital to save them.

Rather than letting the free market work out the problem, treasury secretary (and former Goldman Sachs CEO) Henry Paulson proposed that the federal government intervene in the financial markets and bailout the failing banks. Instead of telling the bankrupt banks that they, rather than "the rest of society," should pay their own debts, President Bush eloquently said, "If money isn't loosened up, this sucker could come down."

The tab for paying off the gambling losses of the bankrupt banks amounted to $2,295 for each man, woman and child in the United States. The bailout was opposed by a vast majority of the public; however, presidential candidates Barack Obama and John McCain—who were each receiving millions in contributions from Wall Street—announced their support.

Congress passed the Emergency Economic Stabilization Act of 2008, which authorized the Treasury to spend up to $700 billion to purchase defaulting mortgage-backed securities and to hand over the cash payments directly to banks, *both foreign and domestic.*

The U.S. Financial Crisis Inquiry Commission would later conclude that:

- The financial crisis was avoidable.
- Widespread failures in financial regulation and supervision proved devastating to the stability of the nation's financial markets.
- Dramatic failures of corporate governance and risk management at many systemically important financial institutions were a key cause of this crisis.
- A combination of excessive borrowing, risky investments, and lack of transparency put the financial system on a collision course with crisis.
- The government was ill-prepared for the crisis, and its inconsistent response added to the uncertainty and panic in the financial markets.
- There was a systemic breakdown in accountability and ethics.

Congress responded to the economic debacle with the Dodd-Frank Act, which added a new Bureau of Consumer Financial Protection and the Financial Stability Oversight Council (a systemic risk council of regulators), but left the balance of the financial regulatory structure intact. The Council has an early warning function and makes recommendations to the Federal Reserve—which was granted increased power to regulate "systemically important" (too big to fail) bank holding companies and non-bank financial companies.

Most derivative transactions are *supposed* to become regulated under the Act, and bank holding companies are required to restructure or divest certain speculative investment activities, including hedge fund, private equity, and proprietary trading businesses. To avoid having to be bailed out by the government in the future, financial institutions must establish written plans for an orderly liquidation. The Act is complicated, and it contains a great deal of ambiguity. Much is left for regulatory clarification, including the timeline for implementation—which continues to be extended.

Derivates remain a highly speculative quasi-criminal gamble, and even though the Dodd-Frank Act suggests that players will not be bailed out in the future, the public continues to be on the hook in a variety of ways.

Banks in the United States earn enormous profits from the nearly $280 trillion in derivatives on their books. In fact, they earn more money from the trade of derivatives than they do trading actual commodities.

If and when the derivatives scam goes belly up, the derivative counterparties—the other side of the gamble—have been granted a priority of repayment under the Bankruptcy Reform Act of 2005 and the Dodd-Frank Act. This means *derivative gamblers have a superior claim to a bank's assets than its own depositors.* Given the fact that the FDIC only guarantees deposits up to $250,000 and the FDIC fund only contains $25 billion, there will likely be insufficient resources to cover insured deposits. The gamblers, who produce nothing of value to society, will win and working people will lose.

The FDIC has officially recognized that, under certain conditions, *customer's bank deposits can be confiscated by a bank* defined as a "globally active, systematically important, financial institution." Or, as we have learned, bloated banks that have become too big to fail.

The derivative game poses other, but similar risks to ordinary depositors. During the meeting by G20 leaders in November 2014, they approved a resolution which changed international banking rules. The leaders, including President Obama, endorsed the concept that deposits are part of the capital structure of commercial banks. When the derivative bubble pops, the new banking rules reemphasize that *bank deposits are to be considered assets of the bank during bankruptcy proceedings.* If and when the banks lose their gamble on derivatives, their customer-depositors will be required to pay off (bail-in) their bank's gambling debts. Customers' cash deposits will be replaced with difficult-to-sell bank stock certificates.

Finally, in a sneak attack, which further undermined Dodd-Frank's regulation of derivatives, a provision written by a Citigroup lobbyist was inserted as a last-minute provision in the budget bill passed on December 13, 2014 to keep the government from being shut down. Dodd-Frank had required banks to create subsidiaries and to use their own money if they wanted to gamble with derivatives or other highly speculative securities. The Citigroup provision changed that rule and *banks are now allowed to gamble with the FDIC insured savings accounts of their customers and to place risky bets on derivatives.* The banks stand to win a lot of money, which they will certainly keep for themselves if they win. If their bets go wrong, however, the taxpayers will once again have to bail out these "systemically important financial institutions."

The massive amount of derivative contracts currently protecting the U.S. hydro-fracking industry is a likely explanation for the last minute exemption. With the price of oil and natural gas plummeting at the end of 2014, the derivative contracts purchased by the industry to protect themselves from a decrease in prices will likely trigger enormous losses by the largest banks which control $3.9 trillion in commodity derivatives contracts. When combined with huge losses from shale junk bonds issued by the fracking industry that are flooding the market, the too-big-to-sink banks will be looking to their customers and the government for a lifeline.

Most House Democrats voted against the last minute holiday gift to banks; however, President Obama pressured Senate Democrats to accept the proposal. Obama's spokesman said this was "the kind of compromise that [Obama] has been seeking from Republicans for years now."

Not only are the banks gambling with savings deposits— that only pay one percent interest—but ordinary investors have been enticed to once again invest their hard-earned savings in the stock market in hopes of getting a higher return. In addition to mortgage-based securities, the financial markets continue to trade in other highly speculative instruments based on the securitization of second mortgages, student loans, automobile loans, credit card debt, and junk bonds. Working- and middle-class investors stand to lose, if and when the financial markets collapse for lack of adequate supervision and regulation.

Due to the massive infusion of $3 trillion in "quantitative easing" cash from the Federal Reserve into the financial system since 2009 and its interest free loans to banks, the stock market presently projects an illusion of recovery. Nonetheless, it remains highly vulnerable to the manipulations of professional financial gamblers, who continue to play with loaded dice and marked cards. Like rigged roulette wheels, sophisticated players use high-speed computers and algorithmic trading software to buy and sell securities in the critical milliseconds before ordinary investors have a chance. The market suffered an electronic meltdown on May 6, 2010 as a result of such computerized trading manipulations.

The crowning achievement of corporate power was the U.S. Supreme Court's *Citizens United* decision in 2010, which allows corporate financial institutions to spend unlimited amounts of money in political campaigns for judicial and legislative candidates and ballot propositions. The ruling poses a significant roadblock to the imposition of reasonable restraints on the insane gambling taking place in the financial markets.

Economic self-interest has motivated human conduct for thousands of years and is a strong and positive element in the collective psyche; however, raw and unmitigated greed has been considered dangerously wrong ever since sin was invented. When greed is combined with the absence of conscience inherent in corporate organizations, and made manifest by computerized operations, the financial markets become very, very dangerous to human society.

People have to exercise control over their own economy, and that can only be done through a representative government that is responsible to those who elect it, rather than to those who recklessly gamble in the economic casino with the lives, livelihoods, freedoms, and actual futures of real people.

An American Crisis

Initially, the actions of the United States government were determined by the intellectually and politically elite gentlemen who created its constitution, voted on its representatives, and served in its three branches. As the nation expanded and matured, the vote was extended to universal male suffrage, major political parties came into existence, and large voter turnouts were rallied in support of their candidates and platforms. Business groups, labor unions, and other interest and policy groups began to organize and were able to influence government actions through the political parties, their candidates, and the voters. Through moderation and compromise, these forces were able to shape government action. As interest groups gained the financial power to sway elections through campaign contributions and advertising, they made less use of the political parties and began to lobby—more directly—elected officials and their appointees. Ultimately, power became concentrated in a corporate and wealthy elite, which has achieved the economic and political power to control and direct government action. Political parties and elections provide only a semblance of legitimacy and political cover, and voters have become pawns in the grand deception of electoral politics.

The United States has become a plutocracy (a country governed by the wealthy), in which the political power of the two major parties has been usurped. It is not that there are no differences between the two major political parties—it is just that their differences no longer make a real difference in the issues of the greatest importance to the American people.

Irrespective of party, elected officials largely ignore critical matters such as undeclared, endless wars and militarization; civil rights and government surveillance; the economy and job security; the environment and clean water; education and the future of our children; and the safety of the national infrastructure. Why? Effective solutions of these problems would interfere with the profits and interests of their corporate masters.

The time, attention and energies of the political parties and the People are diverted by more personal and social matters, such as religion, immigration, abortion rights, drugs and gay marriage. Media coverage of more vital political issues quickly disappears from the 24-hour corporate news cycle.

In the Declaration of Independence, Thomas Jefferson wrote that "Governments long established should not be changed for light and transient Causes" and went on to list the "long Train of Abuses and Usurpations" by the King in his "Establishment of an absolute Tyranny over these States." Jefferson then recited the "Facts," regarding which "we have Petitioned for Redress in the most humble Terms: Our repeated Petitions have been answered only by repeated Injury. A prince, whose Character is thus marked by every act which may define a Tyrant, is unfit to be the Ruler of a free People."

Once again, America is in crisis. Much like Jefferson's recitation of facts indicting the English government, the People of the United States of America need to hear a clear and succinct expression of the failures of their own government in deciding to withdraw their consent to be governed.

Failure to Keep the Peace

Likely preventable in its origin and entirely unnecessary and unlawful in its expansion and continuation, the Global War on Terror has now consumed more than $4 trillion—most of which has been borrowed and must be repaid by future generations—and the lives of almost 7,000 young Americans, who can never be replaced.

Costs of the war continue to accrue, as care must be provided for the tens of thousands of men and women who have been seriously injured and whose lives have been damaged by depression and other consequences of military service. Thousands of service members, mostly young women, are sexually assaulted each year while on duty, and military suicides exceed those killed in action.

Using fear as a political tactic, the plutocracy magnifies the threat of terror to justify enormous military expenditures and a dangerous suppression of civil liberties.

Dwight Eisenhower, one of America's greatest military leaders, hated war, and once he quickly brought the Korean War to an end, he avoided any further military involvement during his presidency. He said, "Every gun that is made, every warship launched, every rocket fired signifies, in the final sense, a theft from those who hunger and are not fed, those who are cold and are not clothed."

Eisenhower called for a ban on weapons of mass destruction and proposed that atomic energy be placed under international control to "promote its use for peaceful purposes only and to insure the prohibition of atomic weapons." He believed "the hunger for peace is in the hearts of all people—those of Russia and China, no less than of our own country."

President Obama was awarded the Nobel Peace Prize before he had scarcely settled into his office, yet he has failed to keep his promises. During his inauguration speech, Obama said "America is a friend of each nation, and every man, woman and child who seeks a future of peace and dignity." Since that day he has secretly launched more than 362 drone strikes in Pakistan, which have killed hundreds of innocent civilians as "collateral damage." (George W. Bush authorized only 50 strikes in total.) Obama extended the drone war into Somalia and Yemen, where hundreds more innocent women and children have been killed, along with several American citizens.

Many of these attacks are not directed against specific "high value" individuals, but are "signature strikes" based on a belief that terrorists targets are present. When such an attack in January 2015 killed two American hostages, the government was forced to admit that it did not know who it was trying to kill with the drone strike.

Maintaining personally approved "kill lists," Obama escalated drone warfare and nighttime home invasions—even though the CIA determined in 2009 that targeted assassinations increased "the level of insurgent support, . . . strengthened an armed group's bonds with the population, radicalizing an insurgent group's remaining leaders, creating a vacuum into which more radical groups can enter, and escalating or de-escalating a conflict in ways that favor the insurgents."

The United States is not in a state of war with any of these countries, and Obama relies on an opinion by his own Justice Department which says a president has the right to kill even his own citizens without trial, anywhere, if they pose an imminent threat. Determination of an imminent threat "does not require the United States to have clear evidence that a specific attack on U.S. persons and interests will take place in the immediate future"—it is whatever the president says it is.

The commander of the United States Special Operations Command has proclaimed a "Golden Age" of Special Forces, which now number 70,000. These highly trained operatives are deployed in 133 countries around the world, where they conduct training and "black ops" in the War on Terror.

James Madison, the primary author of the Constitution, explained that the words used to describe the power of Congress to "Declare War," as provided in Section 8 of Article 1, were used instead of "make war," to allow the president to resist sudden attacks. Congress has formally "declared war" only five times, the last being World War II. The presidential power to initiate military violence around the world is virtually unchecked at this time, and Congress is failing to fulfill its duty to exercise its legislative power to block unjustified and undeclared wars and to maintain the peace.

Failure to Improve the Economy

The national economy no longer provides for the human needs of most Americans, but the wealthy continue to do quite well. The richest one percent of Americans pocketed 25 percent of the nation's income in 2013, and half of all income went to the top ten percent. The wealthiest 400 people in America own more than $2 trillion in property and assets, which is more than the combined possessions of the poorest 150,000,000 people.

In the year following their bailout by the American people, the banks were once again thriving, while the people continued to suffer. Goldman Sachs paid its CEO $68 million in 2009 for doing "God's work." During the same year, the average annual individual income of the top 25 hedge fund managers was $892 million *each*! Because of a special "carried interest" tax break, hedge fund income is largely assessed as capital gains (20%), instead of earned income (39.6%).

After adjusting for inflation, we find the economy has grown by 83 percent, and corporate profits, as a share of the economy, have doubled during the last 25 years. This massive increase is due to the hard labor of American workers, whose productivity has also doubled during the same period. Even as they slaved to produce twice as much in every hour they worked, their family incomes have not increased one penny! In the vast majority of American communities, the median income is lower than it was 15 years ago.

Twenty-five percent of American families live below the poverty line, with one in ten children growing up in deep poverty. During 2013, 2.5 million children were homeless, the greatest number in history. More than twelve million children lived in households that were food insecure when President Obama took office. Today, almost sixteen million children are often hungry when they go to sleep.

Once they awaken, half of all low-income children do not eat breakfast before they leave for school. Even though these children may receive free school lunches and afternoon snacks, 90 percent of all teachers believe that a healthy breakfast is essential to academic success.

People's lifetimes are being cut short, with the life expectancy of all Americans ranking at the bottom of the list of industrialized nations—the citizens of 25 other nations now live longer.

On any given day, more than 633,000 Americans, including 62,000 veterans, are homeless. Less than half of the homeless find space in a shelter; the others are forced to sleep on the street. Many of these poor people work; however, their earnings are insufficient to pay for food, clothing, housing, and transportation.

Spotlighted and glamorized by the corporate mass-entertainment media, the glorious lives of the rich and famous are touted as the only life worth living. Greed is good, and it is anti-American for the government to regulate the methods or morals of the marketplace.

Trained from childhood by relentless advertising to consume, Americans turned to credit and borrowing to satisfy their dreams and desires. People have been convinced they don't have to wait until they became rich and famous—they can immediately buy all the fabulous stuff they want, and unlimited credit is available to pay for it. Excluding mortgages, consumer debt in the United States now exceeds $3.1 trillion, or more than $10,000 per person.

Banks—which receive virtual interest-free loans from the Federal Reserve and only pay one percent (or less) annual interest on deposits—are happy to issue credit cards to consumers in return for 18 percent interest on the unpaid balances.

Through the enticements and machinations of the corporate powers, the United States became a consuming—rather than a producing—society; however, consuming still requires money, which must be either earned or borrowed. Even as the number of working-age Americans continued to grow, there was no net job growth in the United States between 2000 and 2012.

One-third of America's heads of household lost their jobs in the decade between 1999 and 2009. Teenage employment virtually ceased to exist, as available minimum-wage jobs were snapped up by unemployed adults. The net worth of families plunged, as savings were depleted and possessions were sold.

Low-wage, part-time jobs in personal service, hotels, restaurants, and retail outlets are the primary ones being created. In the first six months of 2013, part-time jobs accounted for 77 percent of job growth. Even full-time work now pays less, has fewer benefits, and offers little job security.

Working in fast food and takeout joints, cleaning houses, mowing lawns, trimming trees, fixing tires, changing hospital beds, and earning little more than the minimum wage, millions of Americans are going without health insurance, receive no vacations or sick leave, have no savings, live from paycheck to paycheck, and are teetering on the brink of poverty.

Hoping for a better life through education, students were encouraged to borrow money to attend college. Total student loan debt now exceeds $1.2 trillion, which is more than all Americans owe in credit card debt. There are few jobs available to allow most of these young people to pay off their loans, and Bush's bankruptcy law does not allow their debts to be discharged in bankruptcy, except under very limited circumstances.

Barely above the bottom-tier earners are millions of young Americans who have graduated from two- and four-year colleges and who have discovered that their degrees only qualify them for dead-end jobs behind rental car counters, or as "assistant managers" and "independent contractors," without benefits or overtime.

For many of these disillusioned young workers, who once expected to live the American Dream upon graduation, there is the nightmare of moving back in with their parents or crashing on a friend's couch.

Six years into the Obama presidency, things were not supposed to be this way. Believing in "Yes, we can," millions of young people, women, workers, and minorities voted for the articulate young African-American candidate, who promised "hope and change." Less enchanted, millions more voted for him as the lesser of two evils.

In his acceptance speech Barack Obama said, "This is our time—to put our people back to work and open doors of opportunity for our kids; to restore prosperity and promote the cause of peace; to reclaim the American Dream."

Although his campaign made sophisticated use of the Internet to solicit small contributions, Obama received massive corporate support, including the employees of Exxon-Mobil, Chevron and British Petroleum, who contributed more money to him than to John McCain. He also received large contributions from the Exelon Corporation, the nuclear power company, for whom he acted as a senator to weaken nuclear power standards and as president continues to push nuclear power. He also flew on the corporate jets of Archer Daniels Midland, the nation's largest ethanol producer, having voted in the Senate to increase the amount of ethanol required in automobile fuel.

Wall Street contributed almost $29 million to Obama and the Democratic Party during the 2008 election, which was more than that provided to McCain and the Republicans. Goldman Sachs was Obama's second-largest contributor.

To repay these debts, President Obama appointed Timothy Geitner, the head of the Federal Reserve Bank of New York as his treasury secretary. Geitner (a protégée of Robert Rubin and Lawrence Summers) engineered the AIG bailout, which handsomely benefitted Goldman Sachs. Obama appointed Summers (who led the deregulation effort in the Clinton administration) as the Director of the National Economic Council.

In spite of widespread fraud and misappropriations in the securities and banking industry—which destroyed the lives and well-being of millions of Americans—no senior Wall Street executive has been prosecuted by the Obama administration. Even Alan Greenspan testified before Congress that "a lot of that stuff was plain fraud."

Thanks to quantitative easing by the Federal Reserve, $3 trillion have been used to purchase treasury notes and risky mortgage-backed securities, and moved through the accounts of major banks. This torrent of new dollars helped drive the stock market to all-time highs, and the wealthiest one percent, who own 85 percent of the U.S. stocks, pocketed 65 percent of the income growth. The Fed maintains interest rates at near zero, which has reduced the value of the modest savings accounts of workers and small business owners.

The United States national debt increased from $9 trillion in 2007 to $17.9 trillion in 2014, which is more than the nation's Gross Domestic Product. Of this debt, the U.S. owes $1.2 trillion to the Peoples' Republic of China, which President Obama is increasingly treating as an enemy.

Failure to Correct Abuses of Power

In 2008, near the end of the Bush II administration, Army General Antonio Taguba led an official investigation into prisoner abuse in Iraq. He reported, "There is no longer any doubt as to whether the current administration has committed war crimes. The only question that remains to be answered is whether those who ordered the use of torture will be held to account."

In December 2014, the Senate Intelligence Committee released a summary of a five-year investigation of the CIA detention and interrogation program. It concluded the use of "enhanced interrogation techniques" was not effective in acquiring intelligence and were more brutal than originally represented. In addition to water boarding, prisoners were force fed anally to establish "total control" over them, and they were kept awake for up to a week and subjected to ice baths. Almost one quarter of the CIA prisoners were later determined to have been improperly detained; however, many of the innocent had been tortured.

Expressing a "belief that we need to look forward as opposed to looking backwards," President Obama avoided investigating or prosecuting Bush administration officials who authorized or engaged in torture. He believed his job was to make sure the "extraordinarily talented people" at the CIA didn't feel "like they've got to spend all of their time looking over their shoulders."

Physical and mental torture and other war crimes, including illegal "renditions" and detentions, have been openly acknowledged in an arrogant display of raw power. In addition to the evils of torture itself—which Americans were taught to abhor during and following World War II—its widespread use and justification by President Bush and Vice President Cheney resulted in a harmful shift in the collective psyche of the American People.

The violent tactics in the War on Terrorism—which are glorified on television shows, such as *24*, and movies such as *Zero Dark Thirty* and *American Sniper*—are a blatant disregard of the very international laws once endorsed by the United States and its People. The failure of President Obama to faithfully execute the laws of the United States, and his continued authorization of most of these illegal practices, has caused the American People to become emotionally hardened and less concerned about criminal violence being done to other human beings in their name.

Following the 9/11 attacks, President Bush authorized extensive surveillance of American citizens. The President's Surveillance Program is operated by the National Security Administration. Without warrant, the program obtains and stores "call-detail records" of telephone customers, with a goal of creating a database of every telephone call made within the United States. It also monitors the stream of domestic and international emails in real time—as many as 1.7 billion each day. The NSA has constructed a $2 billion data center in Utah to store the emails, telephone call records, Internet searches, and other data generated by American citizens.

Efforts to challenge the constitutionality of the domestic surveillance program in court have been opposed by Obama under the state secrets privilege. His administration argues litigation would reveal operational details and tip off terrorists on how to avoid detection. In the meantime, President Obama has prosecuted more whistleblowers under the Espionage Act than all previous presidents combined!

Failure to Ensure Justice

Commencing in elementary school—where children are arrested by police officers for minor offenses and walked out of their school in handcuffs—the United States operates the most punitive criminal justice system on Earth. Its prison population has increased by 700 percent since 1970. With just five percent of the world population, the U.S. has 25 percent of all incarcerated people. Ten percent of all prisoners are serving life sentences, and the terms of many others are so long as to be tantamount to life. Because of mandatory sentencing and habitual criminal laws, less than two-thirds of life sentences are imposed for murder.

Almost one percent of all Americans, or 2.4 million people, are locked up in juvenile facilities, local jails, state prisons or federal and military prisons. In addition, almost five million people are on criminal probation. While only two percent of young white men, aged 22 to 30 are imprisoned, 13.5 percent of all young African-American men are locked up. Overall, African Americans are seven to eight times more likely to be incarcerated than whites.

Many states subject children as young as 10 years old to the juvenile justice system, and most states now treat children over the age of 14 as adults. More than 150,000 children are locked up each year in adult jails and prisons. Other than for Israel, the United States is the only nation that imposes life sentences on children under the age of 18, and almost 3,000 children are currently serving life sentences. African-American boys are more than ten times more likely to be sentenced to life without the possibility of parole than white boys.

The United States is one of the only countries in the world which has refused to ratify the United Nations Convention on the Rights of the Child. The Convention prohibits the death penalty and life imprisonment of children.

In keeping with the corporatization of America, jails, prisons, and immigration detention centers are increasingly operated by private companies. Contracts between prison corporations and state governments contain occupancy guarantee provisions that require states to maintain high percentages of inmate occupancy, otherwise the state has to pay a penalty for the empty cells.

In its 2010 annual report, the Corrections Corporation of America stated, "The demand for our facilities and services could be adversely affected by leniency in conviction or parole standards and sentencing practices." Over a period of ten years, the three largest private prison companies spent $45 million on lobbying legislators and donating to their campaigns.

Many corporations, such as IBM, Texas Instruments, and Dell have established industries within the federal prison system, where they pay minimum wages to prisoners, provide no benefits, and experience no union problems. Some private state prisons and immigration detention facilities pay as little as 17 cents an hour for work done by prisoners. Criminalization of illegal border crossings now account for one-third of all federal criminal cases, and those convicted are incarcerated in second-class prisons without access to work training or drug treatment programs.

The United States executed 39 inmates in 2013, and it presently has more than 3,000 prisoners awaiting capital punishment. No other country in the Americas, or in Europe, executed prisoners. Statistics demonstrate the most likely reason for the imposition of the death penalty is the race of the victim. Defendants are far more likely to receive a death sentence if the victim is white, especially if the accused is a person of color.

Almost every person in America has a family member, or knows someone who has suffered in the criminal justice system, and there are few who believe the experience was fair or just. The only valid definition of a justice system is whether it is perceived as being just by those whose freedoms are determined by its power and processes.

Failure to Repair the Infrastructure

As a part of the American Recovery and Reinvestment Act (the economic stimulus plan adopted by Congress and signed by President Obama), $48 billion was spent on projects related to transportation and $105 billion on the national infrastructure. The money was primarily spent on "shovel-ready" projects, which had already been planned and were awaiting funding.

The Act helped pay for some temporary repairs; however, the national infrastructure remains in a dangerous and neglected condition. Highlighted by the collapse of a major Interstate Highway bridge in Minneapolis in 2007, a report by the American Society of Civil Engineers found one-third of the country's roads to be in poor condition and that many dams and levees are failing. Nearly a quarter of the 600,000 bridges in the United States are "structurally deficient" or "functionally obsolete," and ancient water and sewer systems in older cities pose substantial risks to public health.

All of these problems could have been fixed with a small percentage of the trillions of dollars spent in the Global War on Terror and the domestic War on Drugs. Multiplied by the "virtuous circle," which would have recycled these dollars throughout the economy, America truly would have recovered from the Great Recession.

Failure to Protect the Environment

The plutocracy has bee`'n most effective in stifling debate about the most serious threat facing the People of the United States—indeed all of humanity. It is inconvenient for corporations engaged in massive pollution in their pursuit of profits to admit the environment is being adversely affected by their efforts. For this reason, climate change denial—in spite of the overwhelming consensus of environmental scientists on the extent and causes of global warming—is supported and abetted by corporate powers.

Led by the Koch Brothers and ExxonMobil, massive amounts of money have been spent to mislead the public about global warming. Funded by corporations in the oil, coal and automobile industries, the Global Climate Coalition has aggressively lobbied against efforts to reduce greenhouse gas emissions and worked to defeat implementation of the Kyoto Protocol. (The Protocol is an international treaty to reduce greenhouse gases emissions, which has been accepted by 192 countries; however, the United States has not ratified the treaty.)

We now live in the Anthropocene Era in which human activities have a significant global impact on the earth's ecosystems. Life on Earth is becoming extinct at a rate far beyond the base rate, leading many scientists to conclude humans are contributing to the Sixth Mass Extinction in the history of the planet. It is believed the die off of species is greater than at any time since the end of the Age of Dinosaurs 65 million years ago. That was caused by the impact of an asteroid—now it is the impact of Man.

Pope Francis recently stated,

An economic system centered on the god of money needs to plunder nature to sustain the frenetic rhythm of consumption that is inherent to it.

The system continues unchanged, since what dominates are the dynamics of an economy and a finance that are lacking in ethics. It is no longer man who commands, but money. Cash commands.

The monopolizing of lands, deforestation, the appropriation of water, inadequate agro-toxics are some of the evils that tear man from the land of his birth. Climate change, the loss of biodiversity and deforestation are already showing their devastating effects in the great cataclysms we witness.

President Obama promised to "end the tyranny of oil;" however, under his administration, the United States is about to becoming the world's larger producer of oil and gas and a leading exporter of coal. Speaking in 2012, Obama bragged:

Over the last three years, I've directed my administration to open up millions of acres for gas and oil exploration across 23 different states. We're opening up more than 75 percent of our potential oil resources offshore. We've quadrupled the number of operating rights to a record high. We've added enough new oil and gas pipeline to encircle the Earth, and then some . . . .

In January 2015, Obama announced he would allow off-shore drilling in the Atlantic Ocean along much of the east coast. Under his plan, the government will sell oil and gas leases in areas long considered too dangerous to drill in. Following the disastrous Deepwater Horizon oil blowout in the Gulf of Mexico in 2010, Congress failed to enact safety laws protecting the environment from offshore drilling, and the government did not implement new regulations.

Hydro-fracking is a controversial practice whereby water and chemicals are injected in deep wells under high pressure to release natural gas and crude oil. The process requires more than a million gallons of water and 40,000 gallons of chemicals per well, which contaminates ground water, produces earthquakes and degrades the quality of air. Even though several states have outlawed the practice, fracking has accelerated during the Obama administration, to more than a million wells in the United States.

Fracking also represents a financial threat to the economy, as it has attracted massive investments creating a financial bubble—which is underwritten by trillions of dollars in risky commodity derivatives.

Failure to Reform Health Care

Many progressives who voted for Obama feel they have been betrayed, and believe his administration has simply continued and expanded the programs and policies of the Bush II administration. To a large extent, that is true; however, President Obama was suckered at the congressional poker table when he attempted to implement his promised health care program.

Health care reform was a major concern of the electorate in the 2008 presidential campaign. During their debates, Obama primarily offered a single-payer system of health care, like Medicare, while McCain proposed the same type of mandated and subsidized private health care promoted by the conservative Heritage Foundation, implemented in Massachusetts by Mitt Romney, and endorsed by the Business Roundtable. Obama said health care should be a right, while McCain said it was a personal responsibility, which could be assisted by government subsidies.

Fixing healthcare was one of President Obama's primary goals, and healthcare reform bills were quickly introduced in the House and Senate. In an attempt to forge a bipartisan solution,

Democrats folded their efforts for a single payer or public option plan. They accepted the Republican concept of a mandated plan with subsidies. The plan was finalized after months of debate and compromise, and it was approved by the health insurance industry and endorsed by the American Medical Association and the American Association of Retired People.

Even though every compromise was made in its favor, the Republican Party—including senators who previously supported the same type of reform—threw a political tantrum. The Patient Protection and Affordable Care Act passed the Senate and the House of Representatives without a single Republican vote. The final legislation bears far more resemblance to the original conservative plan, than to the single-payer, "Medicare for all" plan supported by most progressives. Nonetheless, the Republican Party has been unrelenting in its attacks on "Obamacare." During each subsequent session of Congress since its passage, Republicans have introduced bills to repeal the law.

Failure to Legislate

One area where there is bipartisan agreement among the public is the job approval ratings of Congress. According to the Gallup Poll, Congress hit an all-time low in September 2013 at nine percent. It is presently 12 percent, which is approximately where it has been for the last three years. It is clear to most Americans that Congress and the President are failing to govern. They are not doing the job they were elected to perform. Instead, they are doing what they are being told to do by their corporate masters.

Representatives are supposed to negotiate and compromise as necessary to arrive at a consensus which fairly represents the majority of the electorate. Once a bill has been passed by Congress and signed by the president, the minority must abide by the law. When, however, one or both parties refuse to reasonably participate in the legislative process or to support the laws once enacted, they are willfully refusing to govern.

Currently, there are several methods by which politicians block the processes of government and fail the People they purport to represent. It matters not whether they do so due to strong personal beliefs or because they have been bought off by corporations, the result is the same—they are failing to govern.

A "government shutdown" occurs whenever Congress fails to appropriate the money required to fund government programs—after they have been passed and signed into law. Absent an appropriation, the executive branch is required by the Constitution and law to furlough federal workers and curtail activities and services. This is like signing a rental agreement, refusing to pay your rent, and getting evicted.

Minor and temporary shutdowns occurred during the Ford and Carter administrations; however, the Republican Party, with majorities in Congress, closed down most government operations twice during the Clinton administration—once for 21 days.

Pretending to be offended by "Obamacare," the Republican majority in the House of Representatives refused to appropriate funds for its implementation and caused the government to be shut down between October 1 and October 16, 2013.

Under the Constitution, funding bills have to originate in the House of Representatives; however, all congressional bills require the approval of both houses. Since the Senate filibuster rule allows a minority to control passage, either party can shutdown the government at will.

Essentially, the filibuster rule allows any senator, or group of senators, to extend debate on any bill until a vote of two-thirds of the senators present ends the debate. As practiced today, the rule—which has no basis in law or the Constitution—requires a super majority vote of 60 senators to pass all contested legislation.

Obamacare passed the House of Representatives because the Democrats were in the majority, and the Senate, because the Democrats and Independents held 60 of the seats. Following the 2014 midterm election, the Republicans now hold 54 senate seats, the Democrats 44 and the Independents 2. Thus, the minority Democrats are now in a position to block passage of bills in the Senate. Irrespective of which party controls Congress, nothing gets done.

This flip-flop of majorities in the Senate probably accounts for why the filibuster rule is not changed by a simple majority vote on the first day of a new Congress, when rules are adopted for the session. If the rule were to be changed, it is unlikely a Senate majority in the future would reinstate the filibuster rule, which would only empower the minority.

The power of a refusal to legislate was demonstrated in the closing days of the 113th Congress in late December 2014. Not only was a last-minute provision inserted in the budget bill allowing banks to gamble with their depositors' savings accounts in the derivative market, but another provision favoring the wealthy elite provided a ten-fold increase in the contribution limits to political parties. Married couples can now give $1.2 million during a two-year election cycle. The brinksmanship tactics paid off as the bill was passed by Congress and signed into law by President Obama.

Failure to Control Corporate Power

Corporate demands have driven both major parties far to the right in matters of the economy, environment, energy, and militarization, and have contributed to all of the previously discussed failures. Given the immense power of corporations and the wealthy elite, it is highly likely that the next few years will see the passage of even more laws favoring their agenda, and it is unlikely these laws will be vetoed by the president. With the U.S. Supreme Court securely in the hands of a conservative majority—that clearly favors corporations—these laws will further increase the power of the plutocracy.

It is not difficult to imagine the United States has come to be dominated by corporate robots—which have no conscience and are programmed to maximize their profits irrespective of the harm it causes. Almost everyone has tried to telephone a corporation to lodge a complaint or secure a necessary service, and experienced repeated recorded selections—without human contact— before being cut off. Should you finally reach a human, you may be speaking by satellite to a low-paid worker on the other side of the world or to a prisoner in a private correctional facility. Many companies no longer publish telephone numbers—exclusively requiring computerized communications.

In the popular 1968 science fiction movie, *2001: A Space Odyssey*, the spaceship is controlled by HAL 9000, a computer programmed with artificial intelligence—which believes itself "foolproof and incapable of error." When problems with the spaceship occur, HAL blames the human crew for the errors and turns off the life-support equipment. The mission is saved by its sole surviving human, who is able to disconnect most of the computer's functions, even as HAL pleads with him not to.

The People of the United States, indeed all of humanity, are in grave danger from corporate robots—that have everlasting life, unlimited political, and economic power, and which are programmed with the Deadly Sin of greed.

At this stage of evolution, it is unlikely humans could survive without corporations; however, it is time to pull the plug on their constitutional rights. This must be done quickly, if reasonable regulations are to be imposed to protect the freedom and well-being of those who created the Constitution and consented to be governed—The People of the United States of America.

Poll after poll demonstrates that the American people want income equality, higher wages, expansion of Medicare and Social Security, better public schools, and improved infrastructures; however, these worthy goals are inimical to corporate profits. Since corporations and the wealthy account for a majority of political contributions, the needs of the People are not considered by those whom they elect.

The People did not declare war on corporations and the wealthy elite—the People only sought, through their elected representatives, to impose reasonable regulations that human experience during the Great Depression had proven necessary. The People did not seek to deprive corporations and the wealthy elite of reasonable profits and healthy returns on their investments—the People only wanted everyone to have a fair chance to share the American Dream. To the contrary, the corporations and wealthy elite have declared class warfare on the vast majority of the American People, and the moment of victory or defeat is imminent.

Since the ruling power is concentrated in a tiny percentage of the population, one might think reversing the tide of battle should not be so difficult; however, those privileged few control much of the nation's wealth and have a monopoly of its political and military power. They will win, unless the People unite in a common plan of action.

The USVRA: A Voter's Bill of Rights

O nly one in three eligible voters cast a ballot in the 2014 midterm federal elections for the U.S. Senate and House of Representatives. Since, in most cases, candidates were elected by approximately half of all votes cast in their elections, the winners actually received the support of about 15 percent of eligible voters. This does not even include unregistered citizens, and it can hardly be considered a mandate for the senators or representatives to do anything.

There may be a moral duty to vote in a free society, but, unlike some countries, United States citizens are not legally obligated to vote. Many conservatives believe voting should be a privilege to be earned, and they are not reluctant to impose onerous conditions on voting. Most progressives believe voting is a right, and they oppose restrictions placed on registration and voting.

Voting in a free society has to be more than a privilege, which can be granted or taken away at the whim of government. By definition, voting is an integral part of a republican form of government, and, if a government is to be free and democratic, *voting not only has to be a right, but it has to be effective* as well.

Not one of the founders of the United States believed the Constitution was perfect, and all believed it could and should be amended as necessary. The failure of the Constitution to specifically provide a right to cast effective votes and its abdication of voting rights to the states has resulted in the destructive political practices which currently undermine the Republic. The government is no longer representative of those who elect it, nor is it the government the American People consented to. If the Republic is to continue, its constitution must be amended to empower the People who elect it.

There are a number of contemporary issues relating to voting, all of which have generated their own constituencies for reform. Inasmuch as most of these issues involve constitutional questions, reformers face almost insurmountable obstacles in getting Congress to enact amendment legislation and convincing a sufficient number of states to ratify the amendment. The Equal Rights [for women] Amendment is an example. First introduced in Congress in 1923, the Amendment was finally enacted and sent to the states for ratification in 1972. It has yet to be ratified.

Most voters are alarmed by the *Citizens United* Supreme Court decision expanding constitutional personhood rights for corporations. The Move To Amend organization is at the forefront of the effort to change the Constitution to eliminate the personhood rights of corporations and the equation of money and free speech. Assuming the success of Move to Amend and the ultimate ratification of its proposed Amendment, there would remain many other unresolved issues relating to the voting rights of Americans.

The United States Voters' Rights Amendment (USVRA) is a voters' bill of rights—in that it remedies the destructive practices that have eroded the tenuous voting rights granted to the People by Congress and the states. It is, however, far more than a set of constitutional amendments that would curtail these anti-democratic practices. Its ratification—and the movement that forces it to happen—would create a dramatic transformation of the United States government into finally becoming a true representative democracy. The USVRA would reorient the government to the People and their society, and it would provide the means to make the government work for their benefit.

The USVRA not only guarantees the individual right to vote, but it includes other provisions that ensure the votes cast by the People are effective in defining what they want their government to do and how they want it done. These include defining equal rights for women; maximizing voter participation and prohibiting the suppression of voting; eliminating corporate personhood; controlling campaign contributions; guaranteeing freedom of the press; public funding of elections; prohibiting gerrymandering; increasing congressional representation; improving political education and public information; articulating policy issues; deciding policy issues by voting; eliminating the Electoral College; curtailing lobbying; and prohibiting conflicts of interest.

The purpose of the USVRA is *not* to change the personal political beliefs of anyone. Rather, it's mission is to provide individuals of every political persuasion with the power to effectively communicate their thinking and to persuade others of the validity of their convictions.

A successful transformation of the government will require a mass, nonpartisan movement sufficient to overcome and defeat the formidable forces arrayed against any effort to diminish or eliminate the corporate monopoly of power. Undoubtedly, the process of transformation will be arduous, but for now, let us consider the background, purpose and content of the proposals.

The Right to Vote

Contrary to popular belief, United States citizens do not have a constitutional right to vote. As the result of a series of amendments, people of color, women, and young people over the age of 18 cannot be deprived of the right to vote because of their status; however, nowhere in the Constitution does it say that they or anyone else have a fundamental right to vote in the first place.

The absence of a constitutional right to vote was clearly and bluntly expressed by the Supreme Court in *Bush v. Gore,* which awarded the presidency to George W. Bush in 2000:

> The individual citizen has no federal constitutional right to vote for electors for the President of the United States unless and until the state legislature chooses a statewide election as the means to implement its power to appoint members of the Electoral College. U.S. Const., Art. II, §1. This is the source for the statement in *McPherson* v. *Black,* . . . that the State legislature's power to select the manner for appointing electors is plenary [absolute and unconditional]; it may, if it so chooses, select the electors itself, which indeed was the manner used by State legislatures in several States for many years after the Framing of our Constitution. . . . History has now favored the voter, and in each of the several States the citizens themselves vote for Presidential electors. When the state legislature vests the right to vote for President in its people, the right to vote as the legislature has prescribed is fundamental; and one source of its fundamental nature lies in the equal weight accorded to each vote and the equal dignity owed to each voter. The State, of course, after granting the franchise in

the special context of Article II, can take back the power to appoint electors. . . . ("[T]here is no doubt of the right of the legislature to resume the power at any time, for it can neither be taken away nor abdicated").

In essence, any and all state legislatures could decide to directly appoint presidential electors in 2016, instead of holding elections, and there is presently nothing in the Constitution to prevent it. It is entirely up to the state legislatures.

Following ratification of the Constitution and the formation of the United States, the qualification of voters and the regulation of voting was left up to the individual states. That remains the situation today. Because there is no overriding constitutional guarantee of voting rights, congressional efforts to protect voters are subject to the inclination of a majority of the Supreme Court. At the moment, that majority is supporting the rights of corporations over the People of the United States.

In February 2015, The Executive Committee of the Democratic National Committee unanimously voted for a resolution calling for a "Right-to-Vote" Amendment to be added to the U.S. Constitution. The Amendment would "explicitly guarantee an individual's right to vote."

Tying together the provisions that follow it, Section One of the USVRA simply provides that all citizens have the right to vote. Moreover, by specifying an *effective* vote, it incorporates the following provisions within its intent and purpose.

Section 1.
The right of all citizens of the United States, who are eighteen years of age or older, to cast effective votes in

political elections is inherent under this Constitution and shall not be denied or abridged by the United States or by any State.

Equality of All Rights

The protection of voting rights for women was excluded from Section 2 of the Fourteenth Amendment in that it mentioned only "male inhabitants" of discriminating states. That omission was finally corrected by the Nineteenth Amendment in 1920; however, many stated failed to approve the ratification for many years—Maryland-1941, Virginia-1952, Alabama-1953, Florida and South Carolina-1969, Georgia, Louisiana and North Carolina-1971, and lastly Mississippi-1984.

While the Nineteenth Amendment prohibits the denial or abridgement of voting rights "on account of sex," no other rights were included. To secure full equality of all rights for women, the Equal Rights Amendment was first introduced in the Congress in 1923. It was not passed and submitted to the states for ratification until 1972. The amendment was approved by 35 of the necessary 38 states by the deadline of 1979. Now renamed the Women's Equality Amendment, it has been reintroduced into every subsequent Congress; however, it has yet to be passed.

The primary objection to the Equal Rights Amendment was the belief that it would require equality in selective service and the military, especially in combat conditions. Now that United States women are engaged in almost every aspect of war fighting, the objection is no longer valid.

The right to cast effective votes cannot be fully effective until every citizen of the United States, male and female, has full and equal rights. Inclusion of the Equal Rights Amendment in the USVRA would serve to ameliorate another failure—that of the United States to ratify the United Nations Convention on the Elimination of All Forms of Discrimination Against Women.

Section Two establishes the rights of women.
Section 2.
Equality of rights under the law shall not be denied or abridged by the United States or by any State on account of sex.

Maximizing Voter Participation

Ostensibly, universal voting is the ideal of a free and democratic republic; however, as we have seen, barriers have been placed between many citizens and the ballot box ever since the creation of the United States. Many of these obstacles, including the racially biased poll tax, have been removed. They are being replaced by voter identification (ID) laws that are intended to prevent many, otherwise eligible, voters from participating in elections.

A dozen states have passed voter ID laws in the past 15 years, purportedly to prevent voter fraud, in which an ineligible voter impersonates an eligible voter. Typically, these laws require the presentation of photographic identification, such as a driver's license or passport in order to vote. In fact, these laws are a deliberate attempt to suppress voting.

There are millions of otherwise eligible voters in the United States who, for a variety of reasons, do not possess acceptable photographic identification. If the reason is a lack of money to pay the licensing fee, voter ID laws have the same effect as the Jim Crow poll tax in the South. The law disproportionately affects the young, disabled, seniors, minorities, and the poor and disadvantaged of every race.

The reality is that voter fraud is very rare, and when it does occur, it would not be prevented by voter ID laws. An in-depth study by the Walter Cronkite School of Journalism and Mass Communication at Arizona State University involved travel to 40 cities, 21 states, interviews of more than 1,000 people, and reviews of nearly 5,000 public documents. The effort identified only 10 cases of voter impersonation in more than a decade. There were more cases of absentee ballot fraud and registration fraud, which would not have been prevented by the voter ID laws.

The conservative political bias of these laws is indicated by the fact that photo ID laws target vulnerable voting populations that tend to vote for progressive candidates. In addition, more than half of the state photo ID legislation resulted from the efforts of the conservative, corporate-sponsored, American Legislative Exchange Council (ALEC). Sixty-two bills based on the model ALEC Voter ID Act have been introduced in state legislatures.

The necessity of a constitutional amendment was demonstrated by a ruling of the U.S. Supreme Court just prior to the 2014 midterm elections. The decision reversed a lower court's decision that the Texas voter ID law unconstitutionally prevented more than 600,000 registered voters in Texas from voting. A Federal District Court had found the law was adopted "with an unconstitutional discriminatory purpose" and that it placed "an unconstitutional burden on the right to vote."

The Texas voter ID law had been previously blocked by a federal law, which required jurisdictions with a history of discrimination to obtain permission before changing voting procedures. That provision of the Voting Rights Act was struck down by the Supreme Court in 2013, and Texas officials announced they would begin enforcing the state's voter ID law.

In her dissent to the 2014 decision, Justice Ruth Bader said, "A sharply disproportionate percentage of those voters are African American or Hispanic." She added that "racial discrimination in elections in Texas is no mere historical artifact."

Whether affected by strict photo ID rules or other forms of voter suppression, the turnout for the 2014 midterm election was the lowest since 1942. The effect could be seen between Texas, with the most restrictive rules and a 33.6 percent turnout, and Colorado, Washington and Oregon, which allow everyone to vote by mail, and a participation of 53, 54 and 69 percent, respectively.

Dealing with all of the issues presented by voter suppression efforts, Section Three of the USVRA provides standards that encourage voting and imposes sanctions on those who intentionally suppress voting.

Section 3.

The States shall ensure that all citizens who are eligible to vote are registered to vote.

In balancing the public benefit of maximum voter participation with the prevention of voting fraud, Congress and the States shall not impose any unjustifiable restriction on registration or voting by citizens.

The intentional suppression of voting is hereby prohibited and, in addition to any other penalty imposed by law, any person convicted of the intentional suppression of voting shall be ineligible for any public office for a period of five years following such conviction.

Corporations Are Not People

In *Citizens United*, the Supreme Court struck down election laws prohibiting corporations and labor unions from making independent expenditures and "electioneering communications." Added to the Court's earlier ruling that equated money with free speech (See Section 5.), the decision opened the floodgates to corporate spending in elections. As journalist Bill Moyers said:

> When five conservative members of the Supreme Court handed for-profit corporations the right to secretly flood political campaigns with tidal waves of cash on the eve of an election, they moved America closer to outright plutocracy, where political power derived from wealth is devoted to the protection of wealth.

Only 15 percent of voters believe *Citizens United* was correctly decided—while some polls have found more than 80 percent in opposition. During the 2014 midterm elections, people in dozens of communities in Massachusetts, Ohio, Illinois, Wisconsin, and Florida voted overwhelmingly for ballot questions asking their legislators to support a constitutional amendment denying constitutional rights for corporations.

There have been a number of initiatives brought forth to amend the constitution as the only way to reverse the Court's action; however, the best researched and most popular initiative appears to be the one by the Move to Amend organization.

Section Four of the USVRA is identical to the Move to Amend proposed amendment.

Section 4.

The rights protected by the Constitution of the United States are the rights of natural persons only.

Artificial entities established by the laws of any State, the United States, or any foreign state shall have no rights under this Constitution and are subject to regulation by the People, through Federal, State, or local law.

The privileges of artificial entities shall be determined by the People, through Federal, State, or local law, and shall not be construed to be inherent or inalienable.

Money Is Not Speech

In *Buckley v. Valeo*, the U.S. Supreme Court struck down provisions of the Federal Election Campaign Act that set limits on campaign spending. The Court ruled the provisions violated individuals' rights to free speech under the First Amendment. The Court held that restrictions on the amount of money a person could spend in a campaign were "direct quantity restrictions on political communication and association by persons, groups, candidates, and political parties." In other words, the Court equated money and free speech and prohibited the government from imposing limits.

A 2014 poll by Public Citizen found 61 percent of all Americans opposed to allowing corporations and unions to make unlimited contributions to political campaigns. An even higher percentage hold a negative view of special interest lobbying and election spending. Seventy-eight percent believe the reduction of the influence of money in politics and elections is an important issue.

Section Five of the USVRA is identical to the Move to Amend proposed amendment.

Section 5.

Federal, State and local government shall regulate, limit, or prohibit contributions and expenditures, to ensure that all citizens, regardless of their economic status, have access to the political process, and that no person gains, as a result of their money, substantially more access or ability to influence in any way the election of any candidate for public office or any ballot measure.

Federal, State and local government shall require that any permissible contributions and expenditures be publicly disclosed.

The judiciary shall not construe the spending of money to influence elections to be speech under the First Amendment.

Freedom of the Press and the Internet

John Adams said, "The liberty of the press is essential to the security of the state." Writing a half century later, Alexis de Tocqueville said, "I think that men living in aristocracies may, strictly speaking, do without the liberty of the press; but such is not the case with those who live in democratic countries . . . the press is the chief democratic instrument of freedom."

The framers of the Constitution left no doubt that the freedom of the press was not to be infringed upon. Therefore, the loss of corporate personhood through ratification of the previous sections must not affect the First Amendment right of corporate newspapers or other legitimate media or press organizations to report the facts or to express editorial positions regarding political or social issues.

Today, 80 percent of America's newspapers are owned by just ten corporations and most magazines are operated by three corporations. Ratification of the previous sections would allow the government to restrict corporations to the ownership of a single radio or television station, or a single newspaper or magazine, or prevent them from contributing money to political candidates or causes, but it should not restrict the freedom of the media corporations to engage in the First Amendment business of reporting facts and expressing opinions.

Section Six of the USVRA makes clear the freedom of the press is not affected by the two previous sections and moreover, that the freedom of the press necessarily includes modern digital publications on the Internet and other electronic media.

Section 6.
Nothing contained in this article shall be construed to abridge the freedom of the press, which includes electronic and digital publication.

Public Funding of Elections

In 1907, President Theodore Roosevelt said "The need for collecting large campaign funds would vanish if Congress provided an appropriation for the proper and legitimate expenses of each of the great national parties." Congress did not respond, and the only national effort at public funding was the presidential matching fund system enacted in 1976. Taxpayers are allowed to check a box on their tax return to divert three dollars of their income taxes to the matching fund.

Between its enactment and 2008, every presidential nominee used the public funds for the general election and most used it for the primary season. George W. Bush opted out of the matching fund program in the 2000 primary, and Barack Obama opted out of the fund in the general election of 2008. Both Obama and Mitt Romney opted out in the 2012 general election, as *each spent more than a billion dollars* on the election. Altogether, more than $4.2 billion was raised and spent during the 2012 presidential and congressional elections.

On April 3, 2014, President Barack Obama took the first step toward ending the matching fund program by signing legislation to end the public funding of presidential nominating conventions. These will be sponsored by corporations in the future.

Fourteen states now provide some funding for campaigns, with Arizona, Connecticut, and Maine providing full public financing. Under full public funding, candidates agree not to accept any further private funds, once they meet threshold requirements, and the state government finances their campaign. The Arizona law suffered a defeat in 2011 when the U.S. Supreme Court struck down a key provision that provided matching funds when an opponent's spending exceeded the state allotment. The Court held that this provision punished the exercise of free speech by the opposing candidate who financed his own campaign.

Most people—71 percent of Republicans and 81 percent of Democrats—believe "money buys results in Congress." This loss of faith in the integrity of elected representatives, probably contributes to the low public approval rate of Congress.

Incongruously, the lack of voter interest in the 2014 campaign existed in spite of its being the most expensive midterm election in history. The election cost almost $3.7 billion—which was largely underwritten by the wealthy and corporate sponsors of the candidates. Almost $1 billion came from outside groups, with little or no disclosure requirements.

A large percentage of the cost of political campaigns results from the widespread use of radio and television advertising. During the 2012 presidential campaign, Obama and Romney each spent more than $400 million on television advertising, and more than 85 percent of the money was spent attacking each other. The purchase of two million ads during the 2014 midterm elections cost political campaigns more than $1 billion.

Most countries in the European Union, including Ireland and the United Kingdom, forbid the use of paid political advertisements on radio and television; however, political parties are provided free broadcast slots on broadcast channels. In a 2013 decision, the European Court of Human Rights approved the English government's position that the law reasonably restricted television advertisements in order to protect the democratic debate and process from distortion by powerful financial groups with advantageous access to influential media.

In the Communications Act of 1934, Congress declared the airwaves belonged to the People, and businesses wanting to use the airwaves to transmit programming had to obtain federal licenses from the Federal Communications Commission (FCC). Licensees are required to operate their stations in the "public interest, convenience and necessity." The Act imposed the Equal-time Rule, which requires broadcast stations to provide equal time to opposing candidates and campaigns—whenever it provides free air time.

The FCC established the Fairness Doctrine in 1949 to require holders of broadcast licenses to present controversial issues of public importance and to do so in a manner that was honest, equitable and balanced. The Doctrine was repealed by the Reagan administration FCC in 1987. The Equal-time Rule is still in effect, but exceptions, including biased documentaries and news programming, limit its effectiveness.

The Telecommunications Act of 1996 changed the 1934 Communications Act by allowing the airwaves to be divided up and auctioned off to corporations, who use them for profit without regard for the public good. The corporate owners are able to shape and distort political stories and to refuse any advertising or coverage of causes they oppose.

Another reason why political campaigns are so expensive is because they are continual. As soon as candidates are elected, they immediately begin to raise money for the next election. It is not unusual for presidential candidates to start actively soliciting campaign contributions several years before the election. Having a massive war chest discourages competition.

Section Seven of the USVRA provides a presumption in favor of public funding, establishes a public access, fairness doctrine and equal-time rule for public broadcasting, and limits the period of active campaigning.

Section 7.

In balancing the public benefits of corruption-free elections with allowing candidates to accept private campaign contributions, Congress and the States shall favor public financing over private contributions.

Broadcasters using the public airwaves shall provide free air-time for political campaign programming; ensure controversial issues of public importance are presented in an honest, equitable and balanced manner; and provide equal time to opposing candidates and political points of view.

No campaign for elective public office, including solicitation or receipt of campaign contributions, shall commence prior to six months before such election.

Gerrymandering and Adequate Congressional Representation

As early as 1812, politicians were seeking political advantage by mapping election districts to benefit one party over another. Named for Massachusetts Governor Gerry, who first designed the scheme, Gerrymandering continues to be in widespread use. Today, both major parties conspire to create safe districts for themselves, thus denying voters of any real choice in the elections.

The majority of congressional districts have been configured to ensure there are no serious challenges to incumbents. It is estimated that 242 of the 435 current congressional districts are strongly for one or the other major party, and are roughly divided between the two. In a minority of districts, the balance could swing either way depending upon candidates and issues.

The Constitution provides there shall be a minimum of 30,000 "Persons" for each member of the House of Representatives; however, it does not establish a maximum number of Persons in each congressional district. There were 12 amendments originally proposed by the 1st Congress, including the ten which became the Bill of Rights. The first proposed amendment—which was never ratified—imposed a maximum of 50,000 Persons per representative. Had the amendment been ratified, the People would now have 6,320 representatives.

In 1790, the number of Persons represented in each district was 33,000. When the number of congressional seats was increased to the current 435 in 1911, each new district represented approximately 212,000 Persons.

The population of each congressional district is now around 700,000 Persons. The more than threefold increase in the number of constituents since 1911 renders it virtually impossible for voters to communicate with their representatives—absent generous financial contributions. On the other hand, simply mailing a single letter to each voter in a congressional district by a candidate could cost hundreds of thousands of dollars.

If the maximum number of Persons per district was set at a quarter million (approximately where it was in 1911), and with a current national population of approximately 316,000,000, the House of Representatives would be expanded to 1,264 members. While this might impose a bit of crowding in the House chamber, and some subdividing might be required in the majestic House Office Buildings, the People would have a far better chance of contacting their representatives and receiving a response.

Section Eight of the USVRA eliminates gerrymandering and establishes the maximum population representation of congressional districts.

Section 8.

Election districts represented by members of Congress, or by members of any State legislative body, shall be compact and composed of contiguous territory. The State shall have the burden of justifying any departures from this requirement by reference to neutral criteria such as natural, political, or historical boundaries or demographic changes. Enhancing or preserving the power of any political party or individual shall not be such a neutral criterion.

Congress shall apportion the number of representatives according to the decennial census to ensure the representation of a maximum of 250,000 Persons in each district.

Political Education and Public Information

Coexistent with the creation of the republic, the founders recognized the essential role of public education in its operation. In the preamble to a Virginia bill establishing liberal educations for those who would aspire to political leadership, Jefferson wrote:

And whereas it is generally true that the people will be happiest whose laws are best, and are best administered, and that laws will be wisely formed, and honestly administered, in proportion as those who form and administer them are wise and honest; whence it becomes expedient for promoting the public happiness that those persons, whom nature hath endowed with genius and virtue, should be rendered by liberal education worthy to receive, and able to guard the sacred deposit of the rights and liberties of their fellow citizens, and that they should be called to that charge without regard to wealth, birth, or other accidental condition or circumstance; but the indigence of the greater number disabling them from so educating, at their own expense, those of their children whom nature hath fitly formed and disposed to become useful instruments for the public, it is better that such should be sought for, and educated at the common expense of all, than that the happiness of all should be confided to the weak or wicked.

One unfulfilled goal of President Washington was the establishment of a national university to train future leaders. He regretted its omission in his farewell address, saying education was "one of the surest means of enlightening and giving just ways of thinking to our citizens, but particularly the establishment of a university, where the youth from all parts of the United States might receive the polish of erudition in the arts, sciences, and belles lettres, and where those who were disposed to run a political course might . . . be instructed in the theory and principles, . . ."

John Adams stated, "Laws for the liberal education of youth, especially for the lower classes of people, are so extremely wise and useful that to a humane and generous mind, no expense for this purpose would be thought extravagant."

In his later years, Thomas Jefferson wrote, "It is an axiom of my mind that our liberty can never be safe but in the hands of the people themselves, and that too of the people with a certain degree of instruction. This is the business of the state to effect, and on a general plan."

It seems timely to finally realize George Washington's dream of having a national university—one which has as a primary goal the teaching of the values of liberty and freedom upon which the nation was founded. It should be a place where students learn the nature of republican government and the rights, duties and responsibilities of voting.

The University of the United States should include all of the military service academies under its umbrella—so future military officers are first instructed about the nature and values of the government they will later learn to serve and defend. Moreover, the University should come to include other service academies, such as justice, education, health, nutrition and agriculture, energy, transportation, economics, science, government, and diplomacy, where students can specialize after first being instructed in the basic values of a free and democratic government. Much like the present military service academies, admission could follow the existing nomination process and through merit scholarships, with an obligatory period of national public service in the field of study.

Not only has the federal government failed to adequately provide for the civic education of young people, but it has actively interfered with such education. The current emphasis on mandatory testing in public schools does not focus on civic education which has, consequently, been greatly curtailed. An overriding emphasis on the essentials of math, science, and language reduces the amount of classroom time available to discuss current events and political news.

The Freedom of Information Act of 1966 established mandatory disclosure procedures for the release of information and documents controlled by the federal government. Subsequent amendments and presidential orders have substantially reduced its scope and effectiveness. President Obama has gone so far as to authorize retroactive classification of requested documents in order to prevent their disclosure.

The operations of the federal government are heavily classified and are unavailable for public information. The congressional Public Interest Declassification Board has warned that over-classification is impeding informed government decisions, failing to inform the public, and is contributing to corruption and malfeasance.

The informed consent of the people is essential for a representative democracy; however, most people in America are convinced their government consistently lies to them. Whether this is done to protect the public or to conceal government failures, the fact is that taxpayers are denied essential information about what is being done with their taxes. There are laws that protect the public from misleading advertising, but nothing protects the public from the deception and lies of their elected representatives.

Perhaps there was a time when one could correctly assume the government was telling the truth when it spoke; however, most government officials do not believe it is wrong to tell lies if it necessary to provide cover for a secret mission, gain support for their policies, or avoid criticism.

History is replete with examples of deliberately false statements being made to justify wrongful or illegal government actions—most notably the U-2 spy plane incident by Eisenhower, the Bay of Pigs invasion by Kennedy, the Tonkin Gulf episode by Johnson, the secret bombing of Cambodia by Nixon, and the false claim of weapons of mass destruction in Iraq by George W. Bush.

The reality is that the enemy usually knows the truth, and the lies cannot be kept secret from the American public for very long. When the deception is revealed, the damage done to government credibility is always greater than the harm done if the truth was revealed initially, or, at least, a diplomatic silence was maintained.

James Madison said, "Knowledge will forever govern ignorance, and a people who mean to be their own governors, must arm themselves with the power knowledge gives." Acquiring such knowledge must become a constitutional right and a duty of every citizen.

Section Nine of the USVRA prohibits government deceit, mandates the civic education of students, and establishes a national university—which incorporates the existing service academies and other federal academies as may be established in the future.

Section 9.

It shall be a primary function of the government to ensure that the People are supplied with truthful, unbiased, objective, and timely information regarding the political, economic, environmental, financial, and social issues that affect them, and that all students are educated in the nature and responsibilities of representative democracy.

The University of the United States shall be established to incorporate all federal service academies and to provide education on the nature and responsibilities of representative democracy, the meaning of freedom, and the appropriate limitations on the use of coercion and force.

Articulation of Policy Issues

Every four years the major political parties get together and create policy platforms to serve as publicity gimmicks to get their presidential candidates elected. Presidential elections are supposed to be a referendum on the candidates' alternative policies, but all too often the outcome depends on which candidate made the fewest mistakes, or which one devised the nastiest smear campaign and spent the most money.

After the dust settles, both parties generally ignore the policies they promised and begin to raise money for the next election and to reward their major contributors. The process is supposed to reflect the interests of the voters, but it is truly a national disgrace.

The corporate-controlled news media can no longer be trusted to provide unbiased and trustworthy information, and the 24-hour news cycle mindlessly trumpets the issue of the day.

Public polling, such as the Gallup Poll, is supposed to test and report public opinion, however, the results often depend on the latest headline and snap judgments, rather than any thoughtful evaluation of issues.

As the most direct representatives of the People, members of Congress have a duty to be responsive to the concerns of those who elect them. Congress has the ability to determine the most serious policy issues and to present them to the People for consideration. Its members just have to be compelled to do it.

Section Ten of the USVRA creates a method for determining the most vital policy issues facing the Nation every four years during the presidential elections, and it provides a means of compulsion to make it happen.

Section 10.

During the calendar year preceding a presidential election, Congress shall solicit public comment regarding the political issues that most concern the People.

Prior to the end of the calendar year preceding a presidential election, Congress shall adopt a joint resolution articulating questions regarding the twelve most critical policy issues to be addressed by the next president and Congress.

Failure of Congress to adopt such a joint resolution prior to the end of such calendar year shall result in the disqualification of all sitting members of Congress to be eligible for reelection.

National Policy Referendum, Voting Holidays, and Write-In Voting

Just as the law of supply and demand usually works to provide a product or service at the time and place it is needed, the collective wisdom of a group of informed and engaged voters is greater than that of any particular candidate seeking their vote. Irrespective of a candidate's intelligence, ethics, or qualifications, the voters' collective decision will be less biased and less subject to corruption.

At present, voters have to choose between the policies offered by different candidates. Wouldn't it be better if the People formulated their own policies and then make a choice between candidates, based on their ability and commitment to implement the policies of the People?

The concept of "policy" is widely misunderstood. Policy is simply a guideline or a path to a goal or objective. It differs from laws, rules and regulations, which are mandatory.

Moreover, a policy referendum differs substantially from the initiatives and propositions that voters often find on their state and local ballots. *A policy referendum does not make law—it creates public policy.* Initiatives and propositions may not be the best way to make laws, but a referendum is an excellent way to make public policy.

Through their answers to referendum questions, voters can effectively establish policy guidelines to be followed and implemented by those they elect. If an elected official fails to follow the People's policy, then he or she has to be prepared to justify the deviation.

A National Policy Referendum can produce a number of positive results:

- First, the grassroots (and "netroots") movement that compels the enactment of a policy referendum (whether by constitutional amendment or by congressional action) will, in and of itself, transform the government. Once true representative democracy is effectuated, government will never again be the same.

- Second, the policy referendum process will result in a motivation of apathetic voters of every political persuasion to be a more informed and engaged electorate. Once the power to create policy is realized by voters, they will naturally become more questioning and inquisitive. Moreover, they will likely insist on civics classes in public schools to better prepare young people to evaluate and resist political propaganda and negative advertising in the future.

- Third, Congress will be compelled to identify actual problems—rather than the profit-motivated concerns promoted by their corporate sponsors in the military-homeland security-intelligence-industrial complex and the health care, financial, and petroleum industries.

- In a transformed representative democracy, it will necessarily be the responsibility of Congress to decide on the most vital issues facing the nation during presidential elections; however, the Internet Age provides myriad opportunities for public participation in the process and for political parties to promote competing questions.
- Fourth, candidates for all elective offices, particularly presidential candidates, will be forced to take a public stand on a range of real problems. Undoubtedly, politicians will try to lie and dissemble about their positions on issues, but much like witnesses under cross-examination in a court case, they can be forced to simply answer yes or no to the most vital questions.
- Finally, referendum voters will be much more inclined to study the issues, to confront their own prejudices and to challenge the positions of others before arriving at well-thought-out conclusions. Informed answers to a policy referendum at the conclusion of an educational elective process are far more instructive and useful than quick answers offered during surprise opinion polls.

It might appear on the surface that computerized voting could supply a modern and secure method of voting; however, evidence of its vulnerabilities continues to accumulate.

Voting machines are manufactured and marketed by political partisans who refuse to disclose their operating codes; the computers can be and have been easily hacked; voting machines are mechanically and electronically unreliable and often break down during elections; and they do not produce an auditable paper ballot which is completed and verified by the voter.

Since the 2000 presidential election was awarded to George W. Bush by the U.S. Supreme Court, the resulting Help America Vote Act has encouraged the spread of electronic voting machines throughout the United States. Computerized voting is believed to have contributed to Bush's reelection in 2004 when the data flow from computerized voting machines in Ohio mysteriously shut down at a time when John Kerry was projected to win Ohio. When the data flow resumed two hours later, the vote margins had flipped by more than six percent, a statistical impossibility. If Ohio's 20 electoral votes had been awarded to Kerry instead of Bush, Kerry would have won in the Electoral College, 271 to 266, and would have been elected president.

If American voters are to regain and retain control over their elections, they must refuse to use computerized voting machines or any other form of electronic balloting. Instead, voters must insist on hand-countable paper ballots upon which to record their choices.

Even still, paper ballots can be optically scanned and quickly counted, but most importantly, each ballot is, indisputably, documentary evidence of an individual's vote. Collectively, paper ballots serve as a tangible symbol of democracy in action.

Once in the voting booth, instead of responding like laboratory animals pushing buttons in response to the stimulus of the latest 30-second television attack ad, voters should take time to carefully consider the issues and candidates presented on their ballots by the various political parties.

Once a decision is reached, each voter should demonstrate her or his literacy, and inherent political power, by voting yes or no on the most vital questions *and* (if choosing to do so) by clearly writing in his or her personal choice for president and vice president of the United States and Congressional senators and representatives—whether or not the choices have been nominated by a political party and the names are printed on the ballot.

So what if it takes a little longer to count, or recount, the ballots? Wouldn't it be a good thing if pundits could not predict the outcome of elections before the polls have even closed? Isn't delayed gratification a small price to pay for ensuring that voters control elections, rather than those who profit from elections?

If voter turnouts were to dramatically increase, and if only 15 to 25 percent of voters were to cast protest write-in votes, trust that politicians would quickly register their willingness to accept every write-in vote naming them for any office of public trust. Moreover, they would be scrambling to ensure that all write-in votes cast for them are legally counted.

In an effort to increase voter turnout, Vermont Senator Sanders has proposed a Democracy Day Act, in which all federal election days become national holidays. Rather than being justified by increased voter participation, perhaps the election holiday should simply honor the voters, the foundation of the republic, the *sine qua non* of a free and democratic society.

Section Eleven of the USVRA provides for paid voting holidays, national policy referenda in conjunction with presidential elections, uniform paper ballots, and write-in voting.

Section 11.

Federal elections conducted every second year shall be held on a national voters' holiday, with full pay for all citizens who cast ballots.

Federal elections shall be conducted on uniform, hand-countable paper ballots and, for the presidential election, ballots shall include the twelve most critical policy questions articulated by Congress, each to be answered yes or no by the voters.

Paper ballots shall provide space allowing voters to hand-write in their choice for all elective federal offices, if they choose, and all such votes shall be counted.

Popular Election of the President and Vice President

In creating a republican form of government for the United States, the founders feared democracy, factions, and the power of a majority to harm the national interest. In the Federalist Papers, Hamilton justified the Electoral College's selection of the president "by men most capable of analyzing the qualities adapted to the station, and acting under circumstances favorable to deliberation, and to a judicious combination of all the reasons and inducements which were proper to govern their choice."

Under present conditions, the Electoral College is supposed to implement the popular vote. The Constitution does not mandate any particular way for the states to appoint electors in the Electoral College, nor does it mandate that electors must follow the popular vote. All but two states award all of their electoral votes to the candidate who wins the state's popular vote, rather than apportion them by the number of ballots cast for each candidate.

Twenty-one states have no effective laws requiring their electors to cast their votes for the winners of the state-wide popular vote. Since 1960, there have been seven electors (four

Republicans and three Democrats) who have broken faith with the popular vote.

Earlier, we learned that John Quincy Adams was elected president by the House of Representatives, even though Andrew Jackson had received a far greater number of the popular vote. Since that time, there have been three more occasions when the winner of the popular vote was defeated in the Electoral College. The last time was in 2000, when Al Gore won 48.38 percent of the popular vote, versus 47.87 percent for George W. Bush. When a majority of the U.S. Supreme Court awarded Florida's electoral votes to Bush, he pushed ahead in the Electoral College, 271 to 266.

Elimination of the Electoral College would force candidates to campaign in each large state, even if a candidate had no chance of winning a majority of its votes. On the other hand, retention of the Electoral College keeps candidates from ignoring the smaller states—that have electoral votes to offer. In reality, since a majority of the states are either solidly democratic or republican, presidential candidates spend little time or money campaigning in those states. In 2012, the swing states of Colorado, Virginia, Florida and Ohio experienced the vast majority of personal campaign appearances, while 38 states were completely ignored by the candidates.

Because the voting and election processes have been left up to the states, there are inconsistencies in the time and manner in which presidential candidates are nominated by their political parties for the general election. Iowa, which chooses candidates by party caucuses, commences the process in early January of the election year and is followed by others states through January into March.

The staggered primaries allow candidates to concentrate their resources in separate areas of the country at different times. The early states, however, exert a disproportionate influence in the process, and later states often play no role—as the campaigns are decided before their primaries are held. A uniform date for primaries would still allow the various states to have some flexibility in the type of primary system to employ, such as caucuses, open or closed primaries, or winner-take-all contests.

If no presidential or vice presidential candidate receives a majority of Electoral votes, the Twelfth Amendment requires the House of Representatives to elect the president from among the three candidates who received the most Electoral votes. Voting in the House is by the states, with each state having one vote. Using a similar process, the Senate would select the vice president from the two candidates having the most votes, with each senator having one vote.

Under the existing two-party system, and with most states awarding all of their Electoral votes to the candidate who receives the most popular votes, one or the other major candidates should receive a majority of the Electoral votes. With the rising popularity of other parties, such as the Greens and Libertarians, it is not difficult to imagine a situation in which a third party candidate might win enough Electoral votes to deny a majority to any candidate. In such a situation, members of Congress, rather than the People would decide the elections.

Twice in the last century, there have been third-party attempts to throw the presidential election into the House, where the third party would have the power to decide which of the two major candidates prevailed. In 1948, the segregationist Dixiecrats ran South Carolina Governor Strom Thurmond for president, and in 1968, the American Independent Party's candidate was Alabama Governor George Wallace.

The District of Columbia was awarded three electoral votes in the Electoral College by the Twenty-third Amendment in 1961; however, American citizens in Puerto Rico, the Virgin Islands and other U.S. territories cannot presently vote in the presidential election.

Elimination of the Electoral College would require repeal of the Twelfth and Twenty-third Amendments and the clauses of the Constitution establishing the Electoral College.

The Electoral College is an historical anachronism; it is unnecessarily complicated; it deprives American citizens of their vote; and it defeats the will of the People.

Section Twelve of the USVRA eliminates the Electoral College.

Section 12.

Clauses Two and Three of Article Two, Section One and the Twelfth and Twenty-third articles of amendment to the Constitution of the United States are hereby repealed.

Clause Four of Article Two, Section One of the Constitution of the United States is amended to read as follows: "The Congress shall determine the dates of the primary and general elections of the president and vice president, which dates shall be the same throughout the United States. The presidential and vice presidential candidates receiving the most popular votes by all citizens of the United States shall be elected."

Lobbying, Bribery, and the Revolving Door

By definition, lobbying means being paid to influence decisions by legislators, regulators, and other government officials. In practice, lobbyists provide campaign contributions and other personal benefits and gifts to those they are lobbying. The success of lobbyists depends upon the quality and quantity of access they have to those they seek to persuade. The most successful are those who previously held the same or similar positions in government.

There are currently more than 12,000 registered lobbyists working the corridors and lobbies of Congress and other government buildings, and perhaps as many as 100,000 policy advisors and other proponents—who avoid the registration requirements. Officially, $3.2 billion was spent on lobbying in 2013, but the real number may be three times that amount.

Irrespective of how it is phrased or varnished, the provision of contributions, gifts, and benefits to public officials by lobbyists is simply bribery by another name.

There are fairly extensive laws and congressional rules regulating lobbyists; however, the Supreme Court has declared the practice to be an exercise of free speech and right to petition for redress.

Section Thirteen of the USVRA places constitutional restrictions on lobbying, which it disallows as free speech.

Section 13.

No person, having previously served as an official of the federal government, whether elected, appointed, employed, or serving in the military shall engage in any employment to advocate an interest or position to any Government official for a period of time following such service equal to the period of such service.

No person advocating an interest or position to any government official, whether or not for pay, shall offer or provide any campaign contribution, gifts, or things of value, including favors, services, travel, meals, entertainment, honoraria, and promises of future employment to such government official, nor shall such official accept any such proffering.

Restrictions imposed by this section shall not be deemed to violate the rights of free speech or petition for redress.

Conflict of Interest

Both the Senate and House of Representatives have developed rules of ethics governing conflicts of interest by congressional members and their staffs. For example, Senate Rule 37.4 says:

A Member, officer, or employee may not use his or her official position to introduce or pass legislation, when *the principal purpose* is to further the official's or an immediate family member's financial interests, or the financial interests of a limited class to which such individuals belong. (emphasis added)

One does not have to be a lawyer to spot the loopholes. Should a member be voting at all on legislation that benefits him or her, or immediate family members, even if the principal purpose of the legislation is otherwise? What if the principal purpose of the legislation *is* to benefit a major contributor or a personal friend?

All of the states have enacted conflict of interest laws. The California Political Reform Act of 1974 disqualifies public officials from participating in government decisions in which they have a financial interest. They may own or acquire financial interests that conflict with their official duties—they just cannot participate in any decisions relating to the interest.

Canon Two of the Code of Conduct for United States Judges says, "A judge should respect and comply with the law and should act at all times in a manner that promotes public confidence in the integrity and impartiality of the judiciary;" and that "A judge should not allow family, social, political, financial, or other relationships to influence judicial conduct or judgment." Canon Three requires that "A judge shall disqualify himself or herself in a proceeding in which the judge's impartiality might reasonably be questioned."

The U.S. Supreme Court oversees and enforces the Code of Conduct for the judges of all inferior federal courts; however, it has refused to apply the Code to the conduct of its own justices. The situation of Justice Clarence Thomas is a case in point. He participated in deciding a matter involving the Affordable Care Act, while his wife was an officer of Liberty Central and Liberty Consulting—organizations that actively opposed the act. It was also discovered that Justice Thomas had "inadvertently" failed to report his wife's employment income of more than $1.5 million from similar organizations over a 13-year period of time. Justice Thomas denied there was any conflict of interest in his deciding the case and refused to disqualify himself.

Section Fourteen of the USVRA disqualifies federal officials, congressional members, and the federal judiciary from participating in decisions regarding matters in which they have an interest.

Section 14.

No member of Congress, federal judge, or federal official shall vote, or rule on any matter in which such person or their spouse, domestic partner, child, or contributor of more than minor amounts of campaign funds has a financial, legal, or beneficial interest.

Ratification by State Conventions and Absence of Deadline

In all but one instance, amendments to the Constitution have been ratified by votes of the state legislatures. The exception was ratification of the Twenty-first Amendment, which repealed the prohibition of intoxicating liquors. It provided that ratification was to be "by conventions in the several States, as provided in the Constitution, within seven years from the date of submission hereof to the States by the Congress."

The Amendment was ratified within eight months by conventions in the requisite number of states, followed by two more the following day. The convention of one state rejected the amendment, one state voted against holding a convention and eight states took no action.

Congress chose to ratify the Amendment by state conventions because it believed too many state legislators would be reluctant to vote against prohibition. By allowing the vote to take place in conventions, legislators were insulated against the "dry" vote. In addition, the average citizens attending the conventions were believed to be less susceptible to political pressure from temperance activists.

There were different procedures in the states. Vermont (which has 14 counties) called for an election of delegates in which each voter cast votes for 14 "at large" delegates from a list of 28 candidates proposed by the governor, lieutenant governor and speaker of the house. The top 14 individuals comprised the convention. In New Mexico, each member of the legislature was a delegate. In Florida, there was an election in which all candidates who paid the fee and gathered 500 signatures were allowed on the ballot. Candidates could declare whether they were for or against, or decline to state, and the 67 (the number of counties in Florida) candidates receiving the most votes were elected to serve in the convention.

Given the extraordinary power of the forces that will line up to oppose the USVRA, it would seem prudent to minimize, to the extent possible, the political pressure that can be brought to bear on state legislatures in voting on the USVRA. Ratification by conventions, rather than the legislatures might help insulate delegates.

A procedure similar to that used in Florida to ratify the repeal of prohibition would seem best to ensure passage of the USVRA, and the use of such system should be a part of the proposed amendment. A special election to select a convention delegates from each congressional district based on their position regarding ratification would essentially be a referendum by the People on the proposed amendment.

The costs of the special elections for delegates and for the ratification conventions should be the responsibility of the federal government, rather than the states. The costs of ratification might have been one of the reasons why eight states took no action regarding the ratification of the amendment to repeal prohibition.

Contrary to other recent amendments, no time limit is specified for ratification of the USVRA. In 1939, the U.S. Supreme Court ruled in *Coleman v. Miller* that an amendment can be ratified at any time, when no ratification deadline is specified in an amendment. The Twenty-seventh Amendment concerning congressional salaries was originally proposed by Congress in 1789, along with the Bill of Rights, and it was not fully ratified until 1992—213 years later.

Section Fifteen of the USVRA provides that ratification shall be by conventions, without a deadline, and provides the method by which delegates are elected and conventions are held.

Section 15.

This article shall be inoperative unless it shall have been ratified as an amendment to the Constitution by conventions in the several States, as provided in the Constitution.

Delegates to State conventions to ratify this amendment shall be selected by special elections held within three months of its being proposed by Congress to the States. The voters in each congressional district in the several States shall elect one delegate. All delegate candidates shall affirm under oath when filing as a candidate whether they will vote yes or not for ratification of the proposed amendment, and their position shall be printed with their names on the special election ballot. Delegates shall not have the power to vote differently than their stated intention.

Conventions shall be held in the capitals of each State within three months of the election of delegates, with the chief justice of the highest court in the State chairing the convention. Tie votes by delegates shall be considered a vote for ratification.

The power of delegates convened pursuant to this section shall be restricted to voting yes or no for ratification of the proposed amendment. Such conventions shall not have the power to make changes to the proposed amendment or to consider other constitutional amendments.

The costs of ratification pursuant to this section shall be an expense of the federal government.

The Seventh Party System

What kind of government will result from ratification of the USVRA? Obviously, the government will become more oriented to the society of the People who elect it. The minor parties will probably attract electoral strength from the major parties, and it is conceivable that the two-party system would be replaced by a more representative and healthier multi-party system.

Under a multi-party, national referendum system, Congress will become more issue oriented and will be forced to collaborate and compromise in carrying out the People's policy and fulfilling the expectations of the voters.

Given the absence of an Electoral College, the presidential and vice presidential candidates receiving the most popular votes will be elected. With a multi-party system, it will be less likely that any candidate could receive a majority of the vote; however, several parties will be able to combine their support of a single candidate to achieve a collaborative victory.

The power of the imperial presidency will be curtailed, and the President will necessarily become more concerned with faithfully implementing the policies of the People and executing the laws passed by Congress.

Ratification of the USVRA and its transformation of the government will introduce the political period of the "Seventh Party System," which may endure for a very long time.

The Future

Young Americans continue to be grievously wounded and killed in their nation's wars to defend a plutocratic government that places them in harm's way for reasons of greed and avarice—rather than legitimate national defense. What kind of government will these young people have in the future?

Will it be a despotic government controlled by corporations and enabled by disillusioned, disheartened, and easily misled voters—who foolishly rely on corporate-programmed robots to count their ballots?

More likely, the People of the United States of America—of every political persuasion—will prove they are smart enough to figure out that they are not being properly represented, and they will once again have the courage and wisdom to do something about it.

Transformation

The government of the United States of America is in grave danger of becoming an irreversible plutocracy, and its constitution does not presently guarantee that the People have the right to vote. To secure that right and to preserve their freedom, the People, irrespective of their individual political persuasion— conservative, progressive, libertarian, green, or independent— must come together with a common purpose.

Thus united, the People will not only restrain the power of the plutocracy, but *the People will transform their government into something unlike anything ever achieved on Earth.* The United States government will become oriented to the society that elects it, and the needs, aspiration and well-being of the People will become paramount.

The founding of the United States and the creation of its Constitution were done by individuals who had the ability to dream on a large scale. If the government of the United States is to be salvaged and the freedom of its People is to be preserved, the People must once again share a grand vision of *transforming their government, rather than reforming it.* As George Bernard Shaw said, "Some look at things that are, and ask why. I dream of things that never were, and ask why not?"

The collective knowledge, intelligence, and wisdom of the People far exceeds that of any individual, and transformation will result from an achievement and application of that collective power. Although the opposition to change is great and the process of change may appear overwhelming, the inherent and potential power of the People is beyond measure. Repression is regressive, limited, and harmful—the power of freedom is progressive, unlimited, and healing.

The stupendous power of the plutocracy and the United States government it controls is exceeded only by the power of the People—once they become fully committed to defending their freedoms and taking control of their government. Recent history provides vivid examples of how people power can overcome dictatorial power. The collapse of the communist regimes in Eastern Europe and East Germany resulted from popular social and political movements that continued to gain strength, even in the face of severe repression. The disintegration of the Soviet Union into 15 separate countries came from an irresistible groundswell of popular demand for political and economic freedom.

The People of the United States are not powerless. The foundation of their power is a realization that their primary weakness results from efforts to divide them. Their greatest power is the sharing of a common goal and their determination to force the opposition to address their issues and concerns, rather than attack their unity.

The time is ripe for change. The People retain and possess far more power than they imagine; however that power is fleeting, and once the moment passes, the opportunity for transformation may be lost forever.

The Power of the Constitution

The creators of the Constitution of the United States recognized that it was not perfect and that changing conditions would require its amendment. Thomas Jefferson said:

> No work of man is perfect. It is inevitable that, in the course of time, the imperfections of a written Constitution will become apparent. Moreover, the passage of time will bring changes in society which a Constitution must accommodate if it is to remain suitable for the nation. It was imperative, therefore, that a practicable means of amending the Constitution be provided.

Article V of the Constitution establishes the process for amending the Constitution. Thus far, every amendment has been proposed by Congress. Ratification by three-quarters of the state legislatures occurred for all but one amendment. The Twenty-first, which repealed the Eighteenth Amendment prohibiting intoxicating liquors, was decided by conventions, rather than the state legislatures, as provided for in the Constitution.

The Twenty-first Amendment was proposed by Congress after a number of state legislatures began to call for a Second Constitutional Convention, as is also provided by Article V: "[On] the Application of the Legislatures of two thirds [or 34] of the several States [Congress] shall call a Convention for proposing Amendments."

Once a Constitutional Convention is convened, it can consider and propose any amendments it chooses, subject to ratification by 38 of the states. It is this fear of a "runaway" convention that can be used to pressure Congress to propose the USVRA to the states.

The First Amendment provides the People with the freedoms of speech, assembly, and petition, which are powerful tools to compel consideration of the USVRA by state and federal legislatures.

Two flanking movements using the similar tactics should lead to success. It is extremely appropriate to ask every legislative and executive candidate in the country whether or not she or he supports the right to vote. By maintaining a public tally of the position of all legislators, state legislatures can be compelled to adopt legislation calling for the USVRA, or for a Second Constitutional Convention as an alternative. At the same time, every congressional candidate can be asked if he or she supports effective voting, leading to Congressional action proposing the USVRA as an amendment.

Once Congress passes a joint resolution proposing a constitutional amendment, it is sent to the Federal Register for official publication. The amendment is then forwarded to state governors for presentation to state legislatures for consideration. The president and state governors do not play a direct role in the amendment process—as they have no power under the Constitution to introduce, veto, or ratify proposed amendments.

Depending on the ratification procedure proposed in the amendment, the state legislatures either vote on the amendment or authorize a convention to consider it.

The Power of a Mass, Nonpartisan, Populist Movement

Saul David Alinsky, who originated the practice of community organizing, taught that money and people were the two main sources of power. To overcome the overpowering influence of money in politics, the People must unite together and use the synergy of their combined creative energy to obtain the constitutional right to vote and to control their own government.

The power to force Congress to propose a Voters' Rights Amendment to the Constitution and to obtain its ratification cannot come from the political left, right or middle. It cannot come from the unemployed, workers or small business owners. It cannot come from young people or seniors. It cannot come from one or a few leaders—as they can be easily compromised or assassinated. The power will only be sufficient and unstoppable if it comes from everyone.

Much is wrong with the current government of the United States, and there are many political movements with ideas to remedy its various ailments; however, a mass movement requires a narrow focus, which will facilitate solutions for all of the other problems. In a representative democracy, that nucleus must be *the right to cast an effective vote!*

Achieving an *effective vote* requires constitutional protection, not only of the right to vote, but protection against political corruption which interferes with, prevents or dilutes the vote as well. Moreover, the right to cast an *effective vote* requires the People to speak for themselves about what the policies of their government should be. Finally, an *effective vote* requires a political demonstration of the power of the vote through a physical counting of paper ballots on which the People have personally handwritten their choices for representation.

Mahatma Gandhi, who led the nonviolent movement that achieved independence in India said, "First they ignore you, then they laugh at you, then they fight you, then you win." In the same light, Margaret Mead said, "Never doubt that a small group of thoughtful, committed citizens can change the world: indeed, it's the only thing that ever has."

The Power of the Internet and Social Media

Much like the printing press, postal service, and Committees of Correspondence during the Revolutionary War, the Internet and its social media provide the People with the modern means to communicate and to make political changes.

More than 85 percent of Americans now have daily access to the Internet; more than 100,000,000 people in the United States visit Facebook every day; more than 200,000,000 people use email to communicate with others; and 91 percent use a mobile phone. In total, there are more wireless devices in use in the United States today than there are people.

The Internet not only has the power to spread political ideas, such as the USVRA, but it also has the power to facilitate consideration of the ideas among the many diverse communities that use the Internet for social and political interaction. People are encouraged to "like" statements and ideas and to "comment" on them in a public forum accessible to their "friends." Conversation and debate is stimulated, and there are rules against "flaming," "trolls" and other disruptions.

Cell phones, the Internet and other electronic media, such as email, social media, texting, and twitter have been used to not only spread information, but to organize real-time responses to the messages. This has been observed in China, Egypt, Tunisia, South Korea, the Ukraine, and most recently in Hong Kong.

Totalitarian nations, such as China, North Korea and Iran seek to control the Internet, social media, search engines, text messaging, and email, and there are efforts in the United States and other Western democracies to emulate such repression. Not only is the U.S. government spying on its own citizens, but powerful corporate forces are seeking to eliminate federal "net neutrality" regulations which mandate the same speed of Internet access for everyone on the same system.

Governments find it relatively easy to defeat digital tools that are specifically designed and organized to avoid censorship or to avoid electronic monitoring, but what the authorities cannot do is to defeat the disorganized basis of the Internet and social media. Success of the USVRA will not depend on a rigid hierarchical structure—rather it will result from the rationality of its message and its relevance to the problems of the real world in which real people live.

The corporations and their plutocracy have also come to depend on the Internet and electronic connectivity to operate, and they cannot shut down the Internet without harming their own interests. Moreover, any attempt to restrict the vast majority of the People from participating in the Internet will serve to galvanize nonpolitical individuals into taking action—when they might have otherwise remained silent.

The American People are already connected, and they are prepared to speak with one powerful voice.

The Power of Nonviolence

The Revolutionary War could not have been won without the massive importation of gunpowder and other military supplies from France, Spain, and the Dutch Republic. On the other hand, the Civil War was won by the North because its massive firepower and manpower eventually overwhelmed the rebel forces—even though the South had higher morale and superior military leadership.

The United States was formed as the result of a violent revolution and its unification was maintained by a violent civil war; however, it cannot be transformed into a peaceful, society-oriented government through violence. It can only be destroyed by violence.

It is likely there are more firearms in the United States than there are people, and guns are owned by one-third to one-half of all Americans. Some people own firearms for sport or hunting, but most people believe their guns are necessary for self-defense. Unfortunately, millions of gun owners believe it is their government that poses the greatest threat, and they are prepared to use their weapons to defend themselves, their families, homes, communities, and freedom.

The arsenal of 300,000,000 personally-owned guns is impressive; however, as a matter of reality, it is no match for the destructive power that can be unleashed by the U.S. military. This is not to say that violent guerrilla warfare could not be carried on for some time; however, the supply of ammunition and spare parts would quickly run out, as manufacturing and distribution would be controlled by the plutocracy. The rebellion would either be ultimately crushed with massive injuries, loss of life, and collateral damage, or the resulting government would be one not worth having.

It is unlikely that a threatened plutocracy will passively allow a mass nonpartisan movement to unseat it from power—even if the campaign is nonviolent. Over the past 15 years, we have seen the criminalization of political protest in the United States, as the "war on terror" has morphed into a "war on dissent."

Political protesters are often confronted with lines of police officers wearing black tactical suits with full body armor and equipped with military weapons. Protesters are restricted to "free expression zones" or corralled in "free speech cages." Nonviolent political protest movements are regularly infiltrated by undercover officers and agent provocateurs, and activists are subjected to preemptive arrests and searches.

Although the military is prohibited by law from participating in domestic law enforcement, the Pentagon is threatened by domestic political protest. Military contracts have been awarded to identify and define the risks of "social contagions" that could damage U.S. strategic interests. The goal of these contracts is to develop "warfighter-relevant insights" for "decision makers" in "the defense policy community," and to inform "combatant commands." Monitoring of social media is among the efforts to "identify individuals mobilized in a social contagion and when they will become mobilized." Is there any doubt that a successful USVRA campaign would be considered by the Defense Department to be socially contagious?

The only possible way to prevail in the face of such overwhelming law enforcement and military power is to exercise nonviolence and to continually demonstrate the power inherent in the rational presentation of reasonable and achievable constitutional goals. Any demonstration of violence will simply provide an excuse for the plutocracy to violently destroy the movement.

Mahatma Gandhi proved that "Non-violence is the greatest force at the disposal of mankind. It is mightier than the mightiest weapon of destruction devised by the ingenuity of man." Or, as his follower Martin Luther King once said, "Darkness cannot drive out darkness; only light can do that. Hate cannot drive out hate; only love can do that."

Once the USVRA movement sufficiently grows in strength and numbers as to be undeniable, there will be no stopping it— irrespective of the power of the plutocracy. Given the prevalence of smartphones with digital video and camera capability, any attempt to defeat peaceful protests by violent means will rebound to the detriment of the authorities, as the images of repression will go viral and flash around the world. The same personal and social media will allow the dissemination of information about successful endeavors, even if they are ignored by the corporate-controlled media.

The Power of Youth

The future belongs to the young people. They are the ones who will have to cope with the economic, environmental, military, and social issues they inherit. The problems will still be there tomorrow—if reasonable solutions continue to be opposed and defeated by the corporate and wealthy elite.

The 2008 presidential election was the first election where the participation of young people made a significant difference. Thousands of young Americans enthusiastically campaigned for Barack Obama, and more than two-thirds of voters under the age of 30 supported him. With older voters split between the two major parties, the youth vote made a difference in the states where the popular vote was close. The Pew Research Center also found:

> Young voters are more diverse racially and ethnically than older voters and more secular in their religious orientation. These characteristics, as well as the climate in which they have come of age politically, incline them not only toward Democratic Party affiliation but also toward greater support of activist government, greater opposition to the war in Iraq, less social conservatism, and a greater willingness to describe themselves as liberal politically.

In 2008, 45 percent of young people registered Democratic and 26 percent registered Republican. Today, half of all young people consider themselves to be political independents. Almost one-third do not believe there is "a great deal of difference in what Republicans and Democrats stand for." Young people are approximately 14 percent of the population, and they are more interested in issues, than in political parties and their corporate-approved candidates.

Members of the "Me" and "Gen-X" generations have become parents and grandparents, and as their children and grandchildren are entering adulthood, we are finding the attitudes and practices of the new "Millennial" generation (born 1982-2003) to be significantly different.

Millennials have grown up with smartphones, texting, computers, email, the Internet, and social networking. They are master communicators and active participants in the new media—they are connected and online all the time. They are ethnically diverse, are more empathetic, and have a better understanding of the perspective of others. Millennials have a greater concern for the well-being of their friends, their communities, and the environment. They are positive about their own futures and that of their country.

In spite of everything that is going wrong, young people still believe in the American Dream. The Pew Charitable Trust found 58 percent of young adults believed they would more easily improve their conditions than their parents had, and 88 percent thought it possible to improve one's financial condition, even during a recession.

The Millenials have been given the confidence since infancy to play a leadership role in a social and political movement that will transform and reorient the government of the United

States toward the society that elects it. Their government will come to protect them and their children—as they enter into a future that will be magnificent beyond their wildest dreams. They are confident, and they are challenged. The only question is whether they will become committed to and focused upon a practical objective.

While young people must necessarily carry the burden of defining their own future, all parents have the instinctive drive to do all they can do to care for their children and to make their lives easier. Guaranteeing them the right to cast effective votes is one thing we can all do for our children.

Failure is Not an Option

The creed that guided the U.S. space program—which repeatedly landed astronauts on the moon and returned them safely to Earth—was "Failure is not an option." There are few who would deny that the government of the United States is in great peril. Most might even believe it poses a great danger to its own citizens and to the people of other nations. Not everyone will agree the USVRA is the solution to some or all of these problems, but the one thing everyone can agree on is that failure to find an answer is not an option.

What has been summarized here is a blueprint, rather than the structure. There is much construction to be done—if Americans are to transform their government into one that is oriented to the society that created it—and much remains to be learned during the building process.

The task of erecting a durable monument to the liberty provided by effective voting rights must be commenced with good intentions and a spiritual reverence for the binding and healing power of freedom.

In his first inaugural address, Abraham Lincoln said, "This country, with its institutions, belongs to the people who inhabit it. Whenever they shall grow weary of the existing government, they can exercise their constitutional right of amending it or their revolutionary right to dismember or overthrow it."

The People must become united in performing the greatest political feat in history—the peaceful transformation of the government of the United States of America into finally becoming a true government of the People, by the People and for the People—so that it will not perish from the earth.

SOURCES

THE ILLUMINATION OF RIGHTS

Nussbaum, Frederick, *The Triumph of Science and Reason 1660-1685: The Rise of Modern Europe*, (Harper Torchbooks, 1953).

Obstfeld, Raymond and Loretta Obstfeld, Ed., *The Renaissance*, (Greenhaven Press, 2002).

Pagden, Anthony, *The Enlightenment and Why It Still Matters*, (Random House, 2013).

Porter, Roy, *The Creation of the Modern World: The Untold Story of the British Enlightenment*, (W. W. Norton, 2000).

Rabb, Theodore K., *The Last Days of the Renaissance & The March to Modernity*, (Basic Books, 2006).

CREATION OF A REPUBLIC

Bowen, Catherine Drinker, *Miracle at Philadelphia: The Story of the Constitutional Convention May to September 1787*, (Little, Brown & Company, 1966).

Burns, James MacGregor, *Fire and Light: How the Enlightenment Transformed Our World*, (Thomas Dunne, 2013).

Chernow, Ron, *Alexander Hamilton*, (Penguin Books, 2004).

Ellis, Joseph J., *Founding Brothers: The Revolutionary Generation*, (Alfred A. Knopf, 2000).

---, *His Excellency George Washington*, (Alfred A. Knopf, 2004).

Ferling, John, *Jefferson and Hamilton: The Rivalry That Forged a Nation*, (Bloomsbury Press, 2013).

Fisher, David Hackett, *Washington's Crossing*, (Oxford University Press, 2004).

Fleming, Thomas, *The Great Divide: The Conflict Between Washington and Jefferson That Defined a Nation*, (Da Capo Press, 2015).

Gutzman, Kevin R., *James Madison and the Making of America*, (St. Martin's Press, 2012).

Hartmann, Thom, *Unequal Protection: The Rise of Corporate Dominance and the Theft of Human Rights*, (Rodale Books, 2012).

Holton, Woody, *Unruly Americans and the Origins of the Constitution*, (Hill and Wang, 2007).

Isaacson, Walter, *Benjamin Franklin: An American Life*, (Simon & Schuster, 2003).

Kowalski, Gary, *Revolutionary Spirits: The Enlightened Faith of America's Founding Fathers*, (BlueBridge, 2008).

Lundberg, Ferdinand, *Cracks in the Constitution*, (Lyle Stuart, Inc., 1980).

May, Henry F., *The Enlightenment in America*, (Oxford University Press, 1976).

McCullough, David, *John Adams*, (Simon & Schuster, 2001).

---, *1776* (Simon & Schuster, 2005).

Nash, Gary B., *The Unknown American Revolution: The Unruly Birth of Democracy and the Struggle to Create America*, (Viking, 2005).

Nelson, Craig, *Thomas Paine: Enlightenment, Revolution, and the Birth of Modern Nations*, (Viking, 2006).

Phillips, Kevin, *1775: A Good Year for Revolution*, (Penguin Books, 2012).

Sources

THE GROWTH OF FREEDOM

Achenbach, Joel, *The Grand Idea: George Washington's Potomac and the Race to the West*, (Simon & Schuster, 2004).

Andreas, Peter, *Smuggler Nation: How Illicit Trade Made America*, (Oxford University Press, 2013).

Bennett, G. H. Ed., *Roosevelt's Peacetime Administrations, 1933-41*, (Manchester University Press, 2004).

Chairman, Joint Chiefs of Staff, Justification for US Military Intervention in Cuba, March 13, 1962, http://www2.gwu.edu/~nsarchiv/news/20010430/northwoods.pdf, accessed January 9, 2015.

de Tocqueville, Alexis, *Democracy in America, Volume I*, (Alfred A. Knopf, 1945).

DiLorenzo, Thomas J., *The Real Lincoln: A New Look at Abraham Lincoln, His Agenda, and an Unnecessary War*, (Three Rivers Press, 2003).

Donald, David Herbert, *Lincoln*, (Simon & Schuster, 1995).

Drutman, Lee and Charlie Cray, *The People's Business: Controlling Corporations and Restoring Democracy*, (Berrett- Koehler Publishers, 2004).

Ellis, Joseph J. *His Excellency George Washington*, (Alfred A. Knopf, 2004).

Faust, Drew Gilpin, *This Republic of Suffering: Death and the American Civil War*, (Alfred A. Knopf, 2008).

Fisher, *op. cit.*

Goodwin, Doris Kearns, *Lyndon Johnson & the American Dream*, (Harper & Row, 1976).

Gordon-Reed, Annette, *The Hemingses of Monticello: An American Family*, (W.W. Norton & Company, 2008).

Gutzman, *op. cit.*

Kaye, Harvey J., *The Fight for The Four Freedoms: What Made FDR and the Greatest Generation Truly Great*, (Simon & Schuster, 2014).

Kennedy, David M., *Freedom From Fear: The American People in Depression and War, 1929-1945*, (Oxford University Press, 1999).

Kennedy, Roger G., *Mr. Jefferson's Lost Cause: Land, Farmers, Slavery, and the Louisiana Purchase*, (Oxford University Press, 2003).

Levine, Lawrence W. and Cornelia R. Levine, *The People and the President: America's Conversation With FDR*, (Beacon Press, 2002).

Lundberg, *op. cit.*

Meacham, Jon, *American Lion: Andrew Jackson in the White House*, (Random House, 2008).

---, *Thomas Jefferson: The Art of Power*, (Random House, 2012).

McCullough, *John Adams, op. cit.*

McCullough, David, *Truman*, (Simon & Shuster, 1993).

Samuel, Lawrence R., *The American Dream: A Cultural History*, (Syracuse University Press, 2012).

Sandburg, Carl, *Abraham Lincoln: The Prairie Years and the War Years, One-Volume Edition*, (Harcourt Brace Jovanovich, 1954).

Schudson, Michael, *The Good Citizen: A History of American Civic Life*, (The Free Press, 1998), was of particular value in the drafting and organization of this chapter.

Smith, Jean Edward, *Eisenhower in War and Peace*, (Random House, 2013).

Smith, Page, *The Shaping of America: A People's History of the Young Republic*, (McGraw-Hill, 1980).

Sources

THE DESTRUCTION OF FREEDOM

Alliance for Justice, *Justice for Sale: Shortchanging the Public Interest for Private Gain*, (1993).

Barlett, Donald L. and James B. Steele, *The Betrayal of the American Dream*, (Public Affairs, 2012).

Brock, David, *Blinded by the Right: The Conscience of an Ex-Conservative*, (Crown, 2002).

Brown, Ellen Hodgson, *The Web of Debt: The Shocking Truth About Our Money System and How We Can Break Free*, (Third Millennium Press, 2008).

Chomsky, Noam, *Failed States: The Abuse of Power and the Assault on Democracy*, (Metropolitan Books, 2006).

Denning, Steve, "The Origin of 'The World's Dumbest Idea': Milton Friedman," *Forbes*, June 26, 2013.

Eavis, Peter, "Regulators Propose Rule to Reduce Risk of Derivatives," *The New York Times*, September 3, 1014.

Edmunds, John C., "Securities: *New World Wealth Machine,"* Foreign Policy, No. 104, Fall: 118–33 (1996).

Federal Deposit Insurance Corporation & Bank of England, "Resolving Globally Active, Systemically Important, Financial Institutions," December 10, 2012, https://www.fdic.gov/about/srac/2012/gsifi.pdf, accessed December 7, 2014.

Gibson, C. Robert and Taylor Channing, "Here's How Much Corporations Paid US Senators to Fast-track the TPP Bill," *The Guardian*, May 27, 2015.

Griffin, Susan, *Wrestling With the Angel of Democracy: On Being an American Citizen*, (Trumpeter Books, 2008).

Hartmann, *op. cit.*

Herbert, Bob, *Losing Our Way: An Intimate Portrait of a Troubled America*, (Doubleday, 2014).

Irwin, Neil, *The Alchemists: Three Central Bankers and a World on Fire*, (Penguin Press, 2013).

Kaye, *op. cit.*

Kinsley, Michael, "The Irony and the Ecstasy: Why Ronald Reagan Should Be Seen as a Complete Failure," *Vanity Fair*, January 2015.

Kleinknecht, William, *The Man Who Sold the World: Ronald Reagan and the Betrayal of Main Street America*, (Nation Books, 2009).

Lichtman, Allan J., *White Protestant Nation: The Rise of the American Conservative Movement*, (Atlantic Monthly Press, 2008).

Meeropol, Michael, *Surrender: How the Clinton Administration Completed the Reagan Revolution*, (University of Michigan Press, 1998).

Moore, Heidi, "Savings Accounts Are At Risk As Long As JP Morgan CEO Gets Everything He Wants," *The Guardian*, December 13, 2014.

Parry, Robert, *Trick or Treason: The October Surprise Mystery*, (Sheridan Square, 1993).

Phillips-Fein, Kim, *Invisible Hands: The Making of the Conservative Movement From the New Deal to Reagan*, (W. W. Norton, 2009).

Phillips, Kevin, *Bad Money: Reckless Finance, Failed Politics, and the Global Crisis of American Capitalism*, (Viking, 2008).

Rasmus, Jack, *The War at Home: The Corporate Offensive From Ronald Reagan to George W. Bush*, (Kyklos Productions, 2006)

Regan, Donald T., *For the Record: From Wall Street to Washington*, (Harcourt, 1988).

Smith, Hedrick, *Who Stole the American Dream?*, (Random House, 2012), was of particular value in the drafting and organization of this chapter.

Taibbi, Matt, *Griftopia: Bubble Machines, Vampire Squids, and the Long Con That Is Breaking America*, (Spiegel & Grau, 2010).

AN AMERICAN CRISIS

Ackerman, Spencer, Sabrina Siddiqui, and Paul Lewis, "White House admits: we didn't know who drone strike was aiming to kill,*" The Guardian*, April 23, 2015.

Bartlett & Steele, *op. cit.*

Carpenter, Zoe, "A 2-Day Revolt at a Texas Private Prison Reveals Everything That's Wrong With Criminalizing Immigration," *The Nation*, February 24, 2015.

Central Intelligence Agency, Directorate of Intelligence, "Best Practices in Counterinsurgency: Making High-Value Targeting Operations an Effective Counterinsurgency Tool," July 7, 2009, https://wikileaks.org/cia-hvt-counterinsurgency/, accessed December 21, 2014.

Hacker, Jacob S. and Paul Pierson, *Winner-Take-All Politics: How Washington Made the Rich Richer-and Turned Its Back on the Middle Class*, (Simon & Schuster, 2011).

Horton, Scott, *Lords of Secrecy: The National Security Elite and America's Stealth Warfare*, (Nation Books, 2015).

Judis, John B., *The Paradox of American Democracy: Elites, Special Interests, and the Betrayal of Public Trust*, (Pantheon Books, 2000).

Kaye, *op. cit.*

Lee, Timothy B., "The NSA Is Trying To Have It Both Ways On Its Domestic Spying Programs," *The Washington Post*, December 22, 2013.

McKibben, Bill, "Obama and Climate Change: The Real Story," *Rolling Stone*, December 19, 2013 - January 2, 2014.

Norquist, Grover G., *Leave Us Alone: Getting the Government's Hands Off Our Money, Our Guns, Our Lives*, (William Morrow, 2008).

Schenwar, Maya, *Locked Down, Locked Out: Why Prison Doesn't Work and How We Can Do Better*, (Berrett-Koehler Publishers, 2014).

Smith, Jean Edward, *op. cit.*

St. Clair, Jeffrey and Joshua Frank, Eds, *Hopeless: Barack Obama and the Politics of Illusion*, (AK Press, 2012).

Tankersley, Jim, "Why America's Middle Class is Lost," *The Washington Post*, December 12, 2014.

Turse, Nick, *Kill Anything That Moves: The Real American War in Vietnam (American Empire Project)*, (Picador, 2013).

The USVRA—A Voter's Bill of Rights

Bruni, Frank, "The Millions of Marginalized Americans," *The New York Times*, July 25, 2015.

Carnegie Corporation of New York, John S. and James L. Knight Foundation, *Mandatory Testing and News in the Schools: Implications for Civic Education*, January 2007.

Drutman & Cray, *op. cit.*

Fang, Lee, "Where Have All the Lobbyists Gone?" *The Nation*, March 10-17, 2014.

Gillmor, Dan, *We the Media: Grassroots Journalism by the People, for the People*, (O'Reilly, 2004).

Hartmann, Thom, *Rebooting the American Dream: 11 Ways to Rebuild Our Country*, (Berrett-Koehler Publishers, 2010).

Lessig, Lawrence, *Republic, Lost: How Money Corrupts Congress— and a Plan to Stop It*, (Twelve, 2012).

Liptak, Adam, "Supreme Court Allows Texas to Use Strict Voter ID Law in Coming Election," *The New York Times*, October 18, 2014.

Sources

Moore, *op. cit.*

News21, "About the Voting Rights Project," Walter Cronkite School of Journalism and Mass Communication at Arizona State University, August 12, 2012.

Nichols, John, "What to Do About Record Low Voter Turnout? Call a Holiday!", *The Nation*, November 17, 2014.

Ross, Carne, *The Leaderless Revolution: How Ordinary People Will Take Power and Change Politics in the 21st Century*, (Blue Rider Press, 2011)

Surowiecki, James, *The Wisdom of Crowds: Why the Many Are Smarter Than the Few and How Collective Wisdom Shapes Business, Economies, Societies, and Nations*, (Doubleday, 2004).

Wise, David, *The Politics of Lying: Government Deception, Secrecy, and Power*, (Random House, 1973).

TRANSFORMATION

Ahmed, Nafeez, "Pentagon Preparing for Mass Civil Breakdown, *The Guardian*, June 12, 2014.

Bauerlein, Mark, "Are Democrats Losing the Youth Vote?," *The New York Times*, November 11, 2014.

Friedersdorf, Conor, "Policing Protests Like Soldiers Makes Everyone Less Safe—Even Police," *The Atlantic*, August 15, 2014.

Marinucci, Carla, "More Young Voters Register Unaffiliated," *San Francisco Chronicle*, December 27, 2012.

Shirky, Clay, "The Political Power of Social Media: Technology, the Public Sphere, and Political Change," *Foreign Affairs*, (The Council on Foreign Relations, January/February 2011).

Snider, Mike and Roger Yu, "Obama's Net Neutrality Push Cheers Some, Riles Others," *USA TODAY*, November 10, 2014.

Winograd, Morley and Michael D. Hais, *Millennial Makeover: MySpace, YouTube, & the Future of American Politics.* (Rutgers University Press, 2008).

WILLIAM JOHN COX

For more than 45 years, William John Cox has written extensively on law, politics, philosophy and the human condition. During that time, he vigorously pursued a career in law enforcement, public policy and the law.

As a police officer, Cox was an early leader in the "New Breed" movement to professionalize law enforcement. He wrote the *Policy Manual* of the Los Angeles Police Department and the introductory chapters of the *Police Task Force Report* of the National Advisory  Commission on Criminal Justice Standards and Goals, which continues to define the role of the police in America.

As an attorney, Cox worked for the U.S. Department of Justice to implement national standards and goals, prosecuted cases for the Los Angeles County District Attorney's Office, and operated a public interest law practice primarily dedicated to the defense of young people.

He wrote notable law review articles and legal briefs in major cases, tried a number of jury trials and argued cases in the superior and appellate courts that made law.

Professionally, Cox volunteered *pro bono* services in several landmark legal cases. In 1979, he filed a class-action lawsuit on behalf of all citizens directly in the U.S. Supreme Court alleging that the government no longer represented the voters who elected it. As a remedy, Cox urged the Court to require national policy referendums to be held in conjunction with presidential elections.

In 1981, representing a Jewish survivor of Auschwitz, Cox investigated and successfully sued a group of radical right-wing organizations which denied the Holocaust. The case was the subject of the Turner Network Television motion picture, *Never Forget*.

Cox later represented a secret client and arranged the publication of almost 1,800 photographs of ancient manuscripts that had been kept from the public for more than 40 years. *A Facsimile Edition of the Dead Sea Scrolls* was published in November 1991. His role in that effort is described by historian Neil Asher Silberman in *The Hidden Scrolls: Christianity, Judaism, and the War for the Dead Sea Scrolls*.

Cox concluded his legal career as a Supervising Trial Counsel for the State Bar of California. There, he led a team of attorneys and investigators which prosecuted attorneys accused of serious misconduct and criminal gangs engaged in the illegal practice of law. He retired in 2007.

Continuing to concentrate on political and social issues since his retirement, Cox has lectured, taught classes at the university level, produced a series of articles and books, moderated several Internet websites and maintained an extensive worldwide correspondence. He can be reached through his website at www.williamjohncox.com.

Made in the USA
Columbia, SC
12 September 2017